# THE PANCAKE HANDBOOK

# THE Pancake HANDBOOK

Specialties from Bette's Oceanview Diner

SECOND EDITION

Steve Siegelman, Bette Kroening, and Sue Conley

TEN SPEED PRESS
Berkeley / Toronto

1🟤

Ten Speed Press
PO Box 7123
Berkeley, California 94707
www.tenspeed.com

Distributed in Australia by Simon and Schuster Australia, in Canada by Ten Speed Press Canada, in New Zealand by Southern Publishers Group, in South Africa by Real Books, and in the United Kingdom and Europe by Airlift Book Company.

Cover and text design by Betsy Stromberg
Food styling by George Dolese

Library of Congress Cataloging-in-Publication Data
Siegelman, Stephen.
The pancake handbook : specialties from Bette's Oceanview Diner / Steve Siegelman, Bette Kroening, and Sue Conley.—2nd ed.
     p. cm.
Includes index.
ISBN 1-58008-537-7 (pbk.)
1. Pancakes, waffles, etc. I. Kroening, Bette. II. Conley, Sue. III. Bette's Oceanview Diner (Berkeley, Calif.) IV. Title.
TX770.P34 S54     2003
641.8'15—dc21
                                                                                    2003009579

First printing, 2003
Printed in Canada

3 4 5 6 7 8 9 10 — 07 06 05 04

To Martin Lewis, Manfred Kroening, and Nan Haynes—still and always the spice of our lives.

# Contents

# Acknowledgments

Our thanks to . . .

Everyone who contributed to the original self-published version of the book more than a decade ago: Betsy Bodine Ford, the first designer; Zelda Gordon, who edited the original manuscript; cartoonist Mary Lawton, some of whose work appears in this version; and Bambi McDonald, for proofreading and inspiration. Ten Speed Press owner, Phil Wood, a Diner regular from way back, who liked that homegrown version enough to take it on, and everyone at Ten Speed who has since had a hand in shepherding it along: Kirsty Melville; Lorena Jones; Betsy Stromberg, for this edition's graceful and inviting design; and, most especially, our delightfully supportive and thorough editor, Holly Taines White. Copy editor Carolyn Krebs, for her good-natured thoughtfulness and precision. Photographer Paul Moore and stylist George Dolese, for the beautiful cover photo. Everyone who contributed recipes: Kaaren Erickson Sooter, Helen Gustafson, Ursula Kroening, Jane Lindeman, Golda Meir, and Ellen and Philip Siegelman. Manfred, Lucie, Nero, and the chickens, for eating up all the leftovers from our testing sessions. And the staff of Bette's Oceanview Diner for their dedication to making and serving perfect pancakes.

# Bette's Oceanview Diner, Berkeley, U.S.A.

It's Sunday morning in Berkeley, California, and down on Fourth Street, a crowd of people is jammed into the tiny reception area of Bette's Oceanview Diner and bursting out onto the sidewalk. The wait for a table is looking like an hour—maybe even an hour and a half—but that's not stopping anyone. Some put their name on the list and head off to browse in the street's one-of-a-kind shops. Others wedge themselves into the corner by the jukebox or find a spot in the sun out front to sip coffee and read the paper. Every few minutes, the host pokes his head out the door and bellows some lucky person's name, his signature yell resounding up and down the street. It's a scene. And it's been like this since we opened our doors more than two decades ago.

Those of us who started Bette's Diner back in 1982 are still a little in awe of this phenomenon. Even though we should know better by now, we still catch ourselves every so often wondering whether anyone is really going to show up. But every day they do: professors and poets, students and starving artists, builders and businesspeople, families of all sizes and definitions, neighborhood regulars, and even tourists with maps, guidebooks, and reviews in hand.

It's an eclectic crowd, but after all, this is Berkeley, the birthplace of Free Speech and the epicenter of eclecticism. With their love of good food, strong coffee, and lively conversation, our customers give new meaning to the term "counter culture."

Settle into a plush, red Naugahyde booth at Bette's, and you're likely to be waited on by a cartoonist, a performance artist, a doctor of theology, or a rock musician. Drop a quarter into the 1957 Seeburg jukebox (our first purchase—it even preceded the stove), and you can choose from the likes of Kraftwerk, Patsy Kline, and Pavarotti. This is no ordinary diner.

The food has never been ordinary either. We look at it this way: A BLT is a simple, wonderful thing. But imagine a BLT made with thick-cut smoked bacon, locally grown lettuce, juicy slabs of fresh tomato, and homemade mayonnaise on toasted rye bread from the bakery across town. It's still simple. But it's *really* wonderful.

Now imagine an entire diner menu—from farm-style breakfasts to soups, salads, sandwiches, blue-plate specials, pastries, and pies—all made from scratch with fresh, local ingredients.

And then there are the pancakes. Classic buttermilk pancakes have been a morning mainstay at the Diner right from the beginning. As their popularity grew, we added an array of daily pancake specials like blueberry buttermilk, San Francisco sourdough, oatmeal-raisin served with chicken-apple sausage, golden cornmeal pancakes with smoked pork chops, and crunchy whole-wheat walnut hotcakes with fruit and yogurt. Not to mention crispy German-style potato pancakes with homemade applesauce and our signature soufflé pancakes that emerge from the oven spectacularly puffed and golden brown.

A few years ago, a bit of good fortune literally fell at our feet. Someone on the staff found a box of paper coffee bags on the sidewalk in front of the Diner. We figured they must have dropped out of a passing delivery van. The box was undamaged, so we thought we might as well put the bags to good

## One Room, No Ocean View

Though most people refer to us as Bette's Diner, or just Bette's, our full name is Bette's Oceanview Diner. People never tire of asking us why there's no view of the ocean, the bay, or, for that matter, anything. Oceanview, we tell them patiently, is the name of our neighborhood. Long before there was a Berkeley, Oceanview was a tiny manufacturing town that fronted the San Francisco Bay. Why they didn't call it Bayview remains a mystery.

use. Before long, we had tested and hand-packaged our first pancake and scone mixes and began selling them out of our takeout shop next door.

Once again, we were a little overwhelmed by the response. We soon found ourselves with a second business on our hands: Bette's Diner Products. Today our mixes are selling like hotcakes in specialty shops and grocery stores all over the country. Like our pancakes at the Diner, our mixes are made with freshly milled flours and grains from a small, family-owned mill in San Francisco.

We put together the first homemade edition of this book in 1990 so people could enjoy our most popular Diner pancake recipes at home. This second edition has all our old favorites plus many new recipes we've come up with over the years. We hope they bring a happy crowd of friends and family to the table at your place, just like they do at ours.

# In Pursuit of
# Perfect Pancakes

Pancakes are simple food. They've been around for thousands of years, providing basic nourishment long before the invention of cookbooks, recipes, and diners. So making pancakes should be simple too. Even if you never cook, you can whip up a plateful of pancakes and sit down to a meal that's familiar, comforting, hearty, and healthy.

But then there are *perfect* pancakes—the kind you'd expect to find in the diner of your dreams. Perfect pancakes are something else altogether. They're steamy-hot, light and fluffy, tender to the bite, yet hearty and rib-sticking at the same time. They're beautifully round and evenly risen, golden brown with delicate lacy edges, moist, rich, and slightly sweet with, perhaps, a hint of tangy buttermilk flavor.

When we opened Bette's Diner, we knew we wanted to serve nothing short of perfect pancakes. There we were on the first day, surrounded by all the right trappings: a sparkling stainless steel diner kitchen, a gleaming grill, thick restaurant china like the kind we remembered from the East Coast diners of our childhood, little pitchers for the maple syrup, a batch of buttermilk pancake batter, and enough good intentions to pave a highway. Our first pancakes were enormous, oblong, and flabby—a far cry from perfect. They came back half eaten. Someone in the kitchen dubbed them "heel pads," and we laughed gamely. But we were miserable.

What we didn't fully understand is that there really are some basic principles that can elevate ordinary pancakes to "dream diner" material. These are not difficult principles, to be sure, but they're not immediately obvious either. We've been collecting and refining them ever since that first day. Now, more than two decades and a million pancakes later, we offer them to you in the spirit of Bette's Diner: take something simple and make it the best it can be.

# Picking Fresh Flours

The more basic a recipe is, the more important it is to start with the best ingredients you can find. This is particularly true of pancakes. For starters, fresh eggs and good flour go a long way toward making better pancakes.

Although mass-produced flour sold in supermarkets makes a fine base for many pancake batters, it can become stale during lengthy warehouse storage, and contributes little in the way of flavor. Instead, look for higher-quality flour from a local or small mill. It's often sold in health food stores. Once you experience the difference freshly milled flour can make to the flavor and texture of pancakes and other baked goods, you'll never look back.

At the Diner we love to experiment with different grains and flours to create all kinds of signature pancakes. You can do the same thing at home. Unlike the batter for some baked goods, most pancake batters tend to be forgiving; you can do a fair amount of tinkering without disturbing the balance of ingredients, particularly when it comes to flour. You can generally replace a quarter (and often up to half) of the flour in a given recipe with another kind with good results.

Try using cake flour in place of some or all of the all-purpose flour in any pancake recipe. With its lower gluten content, cake flour helps make pancakes light and fluffy. Replacing a portion of the white flour in pancake batter with whole-wheat flour produces a rich, hearty pancake. Flours milled from grains other than wheat can add depth, color, and flavor to pancakes. Try substituting a small amount of rye, rice, buckwheat, or oat flour. (If you can't find oat flour, use quick-cooking oats, either whole or ground in a blender.) A tablespoon of wheat germ or cornmeal gives pancakes a delicately crunchy texture—and adds a little healthy fiber in the bargain.

Avoid self-rising flour, which contains added salt and baking powder—ingredients that should already have been included in your recipe.

# Getting It Light

A good pancake, like a bad politician, is full of hot air. What makes all pancakes—and all baked goods—rise are bubbles of air trapped in the batter that expand during cooking. That's really all there is to the process of leavening.

There are three basic ways of getting air into batter: using yeast, folding in beaten egg whites, or adding baking soda (or baking powder). Although a few of the recipes in this book rely on yeast or beaten egg whites for leavening, most use either baking powder or baking soda. That's what makes them fall into the quick bread family: they're easy to prepare, self-leavening, and ready to cook without kneading or rising the moment you mix together a few wet and dry ingredients.

**About Baking Soda:** Remember when your first-grade science teacher showed you how to make a "volcano" by pouring vinegar onto a little heap of baking soda? What was actually going on there was baking soda (also known as sodium bicarbonate) reacting with acid to form carbon dioxide. In pancakes and quick breads, this reaction is used for leavening. Tiny bubbles of carbon dioxide gas are trapped in the batter as it bakes, causing it to rise. That's why when baking soda is used in a recipe, you'll almost always find an acidic ingredient too, such as buttermilk, yogurt, vinegar, lemon juice, or even molasses. This liquid acidic ingredient starts reacting with the soda right away, so it's important to prepare and cook soda-based pancakes immediately, before the batter goes flat.

**About Baking Powder:** In the late nineteenth century, someone had the bright idea of combining baking soda with powdered tartaric acid (cream of tartar) to create the one-step leavener now known as baking powder. When moistened, the tartaric acid dissolves and reacts with the soda. Recipes containing baking powder don't need added acids in the form of buttermilk, vinegar, and so on. Double-acting baking powder (which is just about the only kind available in the United States) releases some gas when it is initially moistened and the rest when it is exposed to heat. This means that there's less urgency involved: you don't have to make the pancakes as soon as the batter is mixed.

Although baking powder contains a little cornstarch to absorb moisture and keep the soda and tartaric acid from reacting in the package, it does eventually go flat. It's a good idea to replace baking powder often—long before the expiration date on the package. You can test it by mixing a quarter teaspoon with one tablespoon of hot water. If the mixture doesn't begin to bubble immediately, replace your baking powder.

Our basic recipe for buttermilk pancakes (page 24) uses both baking powder and baking soda. Why? At the diner, we need a batter that can hold up all day. That's where the baking powder comes in. But we also want the flavor and richness of buttermilk. That's where the baking soda comes in. Besides acting as a leavener, it also neutralizes the acidity of the buttermilk, eliminating much of its sourness.

## Don't Batter the Batter

Have you ever noticed how pancake and quick bread recipes caution "do not overmix"? If you want light, tender pancakes, don't take this advice lightly. With leavened pancakes—as opposed to, say, crepes—too much mixing overdevelops the gluten in the flour, making the batter elastic. Elastic batter means rubbery pancakes. Overmixing also bursts those precious air bubbles you've worked so hard to create. Without them, your finished product will give new meaning to the phrase "flat as a pancake."

Begin by thoroughly mixing the dry ingredients in their own bowl using a wire whisk. This way, you'll need to mix the batter less once the wet ingredients are added. In a second bowl, beat the eggs lightly (if the recipe includes eggs), and then add the other liquid ingredients. If you're using melted butter, it's helpful to have the eggs and the other liquid ingredients at room temperature. If they're too cold, the butter will harden in clumps.

Add the wet ingredients to the dry ones all at once. Use the whisk to gently stir *just* until everything is moistened. Don't worry about the small lumps. They will cook out and disappear.

# The Thick of It

The consistency of pancake batter is important—and unpredictable. Your ingredients, how long you let the batter sit, and even the weather all contribute to the consistency of your batter. If the batter is too runny, it will spread out too much on the griddle, resulting in flat, thin pancakes. If it's too thick it won't spread properly, and your pancakes may turn out doughy at the center. When the consistency is just right, the batter spreads in even rounds that rise and cook uniformly.

To thin pancake batter, start by gently stirring in a small amount of water or milk. Then try a test pancake and, if needed, continue to add liquid. Remember that batters made with wheat flour tend to thicken as they stand, so the longer you keep your batter around, the more you may need to thin it out.

Thickening batters is a little trickier because you need to be careful not to overmix them. Sift a small amount of flour over the batter, then gently fold it in. Or carefully incorporate a little wheat germ or quick-cooking oats.

# Griddle Me This

The classic sheet grill is the centerpiece of most diner kitchens. Many short-order cooks use it for scrambling eggs, making omelets, and cooking all kinds of hot entrées. At Bette's, we reserve the griddle for just a few items: home-fries, French toast, bacon, breakfast links, homemade scrapple, and, of course, pancakes. With its spacious, flat, evenly heated surface, there's nothing like a real griddle for creating perfect griddlecakes.

If you're lucky enough to have a stove with a built-in griddle, by all means use it. If you really love pancakes, a small, freestanding electric griddle is a worthwhile investment. It lets you cook several pancakes at a time, heats evenly and is usually coated with a nonstick surface. Because it has a built-in thermostat, it doesn't require constant temperature adjustments. Cast-iron stovetop griddles—especially the ones that are designed to span two burners—also work well.

Needless to say, pancakes can also be made in a pan. If you have a large, well-seasoned, cast-iron skillet, you'll find it ideal for pancakes—thick enough to bake them evenly and keep them from burning on the bottom before they're cooked through. To clean the skillet between batches and to prevent sticking, rub it with a paper towel dipped in salt. To keep the pan seasoned, avoid cleaning it with soap or detergent and rub it with a little oil before storing. A pan with a nonstick coating can also be used for pancakes. Choose one with a thick, heavy bottom and as much flat cooking area as possible.

# Grease Lightly

Even though they're made on a griddle or in a pan, the correct word for cooking pancakes is *bake*, not *fry*. Go easy on the fat you use to grease the griddle. Most pancake batters—all of the ones in this book—contain enough fat to prevent the cakes from sticking to the griddle. All that is needed is a light coating of vegetable oil, brushed onto the cooking surface with a paper towel. If your cooking surface is well seasoned or has a nonstick coating, you shouldn't need to keep greasing the griddle between each batch. Unflavored nonstick cooking spray also works well for griddle greasing. Spray it on before heating the griddle.

## The Heat Is On

Like the consistency of the batter, the temperature of the cooking surface needs to be just right. Begin by heating the griddle or pan to medium-high. If you're using an electric skillet or griddle with a thermostat, set it to 375°F. Oil the surface lightly and heat for a few minutes, then test the temperature by sprinkling a few drops of cold water onto the griddle. If the water vaporizes immediately, the surface is too hot. If it boils and steams listlessly, it's not hot enough. When the droplets jump and dance on the griddle, you're ready to make pancakes. Keep an eye on the temperature of the cooking surface, adjusting it as you go. Or as Bette says: "Fiddle with the griddle!"

## Batter's Up!

At the Diner, we think that about a quarter of a cup of batter makes pancakes of the perfect size (about four inches). They cook evenly and are manageable to work with.

Gently pour pancake batter onto the griddle using a spoon, measuring cup, or, best of all, a quarter-cup (two-ounce) ladle, which lets you keep your hand a comfortable distance away from the heat. Hold the ladle just above the surface of the griddle. The higher you hold it, the more you risk breaking the air bubbles in the batter. Drizzling a steam of batter from on high like a Balkan waiter pouring tea makes for messy, misshapen pancakes. Spoon carefully, and the batter will spread out in perfect circles.

Don't let the pancakes touch each other. Leave enough space between them so that they have room to spread out without merging. They'll cook better and look better. Don't move pancakes around while the first side is cooking. This breaks the seal between the pancake and the griddle, and the pancake will not brown as evenly or as thoroughly.

## Flipping with Finesse

A broad, heavy restaurant-style spatula is helpful for flipping pancakes without folding or tearing them. For crêpes, a long, narrow, offset spatula works well.

Flip pancakes when their surface is covered with bubbles and the edges look dry. This usually takes between two and three minutes from the time you pour the batter onto the griddle. Before you flip over to the second side, use a spatula to peel back the edge and make sure the first side is golden brown.

In cartoons, flapjacks are always catapulted sky-high off the griddle or tossed and flipped from a pan. It's dramatic, but nothing kills a pancake faster. Resist the temptation and instead slide a spatula under the pancake, turning it gently. Imagine you're flipping a fried egg and don't want to break the yolk.

After flipping, cook for a minute or two more. Never pat pancakes down with the spatula and never flip them more than once.

## Sprinkles and Add-Ins

At the Diner, we're always coming up with creative pancake specials, often based on our beloved buttermilk pancakes (page 24). Sometimes we mix ingredients into the batter before cooking. Or, easier still, we simply pour the batter onto the griddle, then sprinkle fruit, nuts, or other ingredients right onto the pancakes before flipping them. If you have a family with diverse tastes or want to surprise your brunch guests with a variety of pancakes, this method can be very handy. Some of our favorite sprinkles and stir-ins include berries, sliced bananas, dried cherries, dried cranberries, golden raisins, currants, sunflower seeds, and chopped, toasted walnuts or almonds.

# Finishing Touches

How you present food is just as important as how you prepare it. At the Diner, we take a lot of pride in our presentations. Here are a few simple touches that can help make your perfect pancakes seem even more perfect.

- *Warm everything—the plates, the syrup, even the room! Pancakes get cold quickly.*

- *Heat maple syrup in the microwave for 15 to 30 seconds in a small, microwave-safe creamer. Put the creamer on a saucer before heating to catch any drips.*

- *Make pancakes all the same size—using a quarter-cup ladle will help—and stack them or arrange them in neat little rows.*

- *Pancakes are more attractive served with the side cooked first facing up, because that side is more evenly browned.*

- *Top pancakes with a dollop of whipped butter, warmed to room temperature and scooped out with a melon baller. Or serve a little pitcher of warm melted butter on the side.*

- *Add a simple garnish: a dusting of sifted confectioners' sugar, a sprig of mint, a few fresh berries, banana slices, or a wedge of orange. We like to garnish flavored pancakes with a little bit of the raw material that went into them: a few crisp slices of apple on apple pancakes, half a toasted walnut on walnut pancakes, and so on.*

- *Don't skimp on syrup. If you're serving maple syrup, treat yourself and your guests to the real, 100 percent pure variety instead of "pancake syrup" or "maple-flavored syrup," which are typically made from corn syrup flavored with maple syrup or artificial maple extract. Real maple syrup is well worth the expense, and a little goes a long way.*

• *Serve pancakes with a selection of simple hot or cold homemade toppings. See pages 102 through 108 for ideas.*

## Maple Syrup— There Are No Bad Grades

Look at the label of a bottle of real maple syrup, and you'll see a grade designation, ranging from AA (or "Fancy"), to A, B, or C. These grades are used to designate color and flavor, not quality. On one end of the spectrum, Grade AA is a delicately flavored amber syrup. On the other, Grade C is dark with a very strong, molasses-like flavor. Generally speaking, syrup made earlier in the season is lighter and will have a higher grade. But unlike in school, one grade is not better than another. It's a matter of personal preference, just like choosing a darker or a lighter beer. Try several grades and stick with the one that suits your taste. Store real maple syrup in the refrigerator and warm it before serving to bring out its flavor.

# Keeping Pancakes Warm

Pancakes are at their peak when served steaming hot, right from the griddle. If you're a short-order cook, this is no problem. You plate them up, ring the bell, and they're on their way. However, if you don't want to be stuck in the kitchen while your friends and family gorge themselves on round after round of the pancakes you have worked so hard to perfect, there is another way.

Layer a few batches of pancakes on a baking sheet lined with a cloth towel and keep them warm in a 250°F oven. Each layer should be separated from the next by a towel to absorb steam. Try not to stack too many layers. You can store pancakes in this way for up to ten minutes. As soon as the last batch is cooked, serve it first on a warm platter. This will start things off nicely. Then dish up your stored reserves, bring them to the table, and join the party.

With a little practice, you can keep two or three griddles or pans going at once, further speeding up the cooking process.

Another way to reduce the amount of time you spend in the kitchen is to do some advance preparation the night before. Though some batters hold well in the refrigerator overnight, most tend to thicken and lose some of their airiness. We feel that the best pancakes are made from just-mixed batter that has been allowed to rest for a few minutes. Instead of preparing the batter the night before, try measuring and mixing the dry ingredients in one bowl and the wet ones in another. Store the wet ingredients overnight in the refrigerator. It's a simple matter to combine the two mixtures just before cooking.

## A Note on Nutrition

Are pancakes a healthy food? Absolutely. Current guidelines for healthy eating point to grains as one of the basic cornerstones of a healthy diet, and pancakes are rich in complex carbohydrates, the body's best source of energy. A hearty pancake breakfast does more than satisfy the soul. It can give you the fuel you need all morning long. And don't overlook pancakes at other meals. Add a simple savory topping or a side dish, and they can make a wholesome, high-energy lunch or dinner too.

It's the accompaniments that can turn a healthy pancake meal into an orgy of excess. If you're concerned about fat and cholesterol, try serving pancakes with fresh, healthy toppings, such as berries, sliced fruit, fruit compotes, or low-fat yogurt.

At the Diner, the words "no substitutions" have never appeared on our menu. We believe in staying flexible and encouraging our customers to suggest substitutions and be creative. The same thing might be said for the pancake recipes in this book. There are all kinds of substitutions you can make to cut down on fat and cholesterol. Here are a few.

- *Replace whole eggs with a cholesterol-free egg substitute or egg whites (two whites take the place of one whole egg).*

- *Replace melted butter with vegetable oil (canola oil is the lowest in saturated fat).*

- *Fruit purées can be used to replace fat in baked goods with surprisingly tasty results. Try replacing some or all of the fat in your favorite pancake recipe with applesauce.*

*This works remarkably well in our Low-Fat Pancakes
(page 54).*

- *Use nonfat milk in place of whole milk or buttermilk—or
substitute nonfat yogurt for buttermilk.*

- *Replace milk or buttermilk with fruit juice. Add a small
amount of baking soda (about 1/4 teaspoon).*

- *Use a cholesterol-free cooking spray to grease your griddle
or pan.*

Of course, these substitutions will affect the flavor, texture,
and appearance of your pancakes. That's why, when all is said
and done, we always come back to basic, classic pancakes,
made with the kinds of fresh ingredients people have been
using for centuries. Eat them in moderation as part of a varied,
healthy diet, and you're home free.

# Pancake Mixes—A Mixed Bag

Pancake mixes are more than just a convenience food. What
you're really buying in a good mix is a good recipe. What
makes some mixes better than others? All good cooking
begins with high-quality ingredients. Of course, being in the
pancake-mix business, we like to think our oatmeal, buckwheat, and buttermilk pancake and waffle mixes are among
the best you can buy. They're made from freshly milled flours
and natural ingredients, and they taste like real, homemade
pancakes should.

The problem with many pancake mixes is that they're
made in giant batches with over-the-hill flour. The "just-add-
water" variety tend to be made with powdered eggs and a
variety of mysterious ingredients that wind up tasting less
than fresh.

Multipurpose pancake/waffle/biscuit/dumpling/and-so-
on mixes are convenient, but they promise too much. Have

you noticed how everything you make from them winds up tasting more or less like a salty biscuit?

We've tasted just about every pancake mix on the market and found that the best are made by small mills, or companies that buy from local mills. These mixes are designed to make pancakes, maybe waffles, and nothing more. They may be a bit more expensive and require a few extra steps and ingredients, but that's what makes them the best.

If you're a pancake "frequent fryer," consider making your own mix to have on hand. Just blend the dry ingredients for your favorite recipe and store them in an airtight container in a cool, dry place.

# A Word about Waffles

Waffle batter is a lot like pancake batter, and it's a simple matter to turn many of the pancakes in this book into waffles. In fact, you'll find that our basic recipes for buttermilk, corn-meal, and buckwheat pancakes can all be used as is to make delicious waffles. If you're feeling adventurous and want to try making waffles from your favorite pancake recipes, you may need to make some modifications. Here are a few tips.

- *You can increase the fat in a pancake batter by up to half. This keeps waffles from sticking to the iron and helps them brown.*

- *Try increasing the liquid slightly to thin the batter. A thinner batter spreads more evenly on the iron and produces a more tender waffle.*

- *For lighter waffles, separate the eggs, beat the whites until they are stiff, but not dry, and fold the beaten whites into the batter as a final step.*

- *For crisper waffles, add a small amount of sugar to the batter.*

- *To cook waffles, pour between half and three-quarters of a cup of batter (check the manufacturer's directions) onto the hot waffle iron, close the lid, and bake the waffle until it stops steaming and is nicely browned.*

- *Waffles freeze well, and frozen waffles can be easily reheated in the toaster or the oven.*

# The Pancake Pantry

With a few basic pantry staples, you can turn out most of the pancakes in this book without having to run to the store for special ingredients. Here's a checklist for stocking your pancake pantry.

## DRY GOODS

All-purpose flour

Baking powder

Baking soda

Brown sugar, light or dark

Buckwheat flour

Cake flour

Confectioners' sugar

Cornmeal, fine

Granulated sugar

Salt

Walnuts, pecans, or almonds

Wheat germ

Whole-wheat flour

## DAIRY PRODUCTS

Butter, salted

Buttermilk

Cottage cheese

Eggs, large

Milk, nonfat, low-fat, or whole

Sour cream

Yogurt, plain

## OTHER STAPLES

Maple syrup

Vegetable oil

Judging by their ever-increasing popularity at the Diner, pan-cakes are making a major comeback. We think they deserve to. And we hope the recipes in this book will convince you to climb aboard the pancake bandwagon.

Perfect pancakes—unlike a lot of other things in life—require nothing more than a little practice and patience. Keep trying the same recipe again and again, and pretty soon you'll have mastered something simple and satisfying that you can call your own. What could be more perfect than that?

# Pancakes AND Griddlecakes

We pancake lovers like to think that the discovery of the pancake actually marked the very beginning of cooking. You see, pancakes date back to prehistory—probably even before the domestication of fire—when people first learned to mash grain and water together and bake the resulting dough on a hot rock in the sunshine. This was no mere gathering of food and cramming it into a hungry mouth. This was preparing and mixing ingredients, applying heat over time to effect chemical change, and winding up with an edible product that had never existed before. It was a great moment in anthropological and culinary history . . . and pancakes were there!

There is evidence that pancakes were central to nearly all ancient cultures, from Greece and Rome to Egypt and China. It's easy to imagine how those first unleavened breads were prized over other foods. Food historians believed that they held symbolic meaning to early sun worshipers because of their round shape and sustaining warmth.

Today, pancakes remain one of the few foods universal to all cuisines, an Esperanto of the epicurean world. The term *pancake* has come to mean a flat "quick bread," browned on both sides on a griddle. Basic pancake batter is made from flour and water or milk, maybe egg, maybe leavening, maybe sugar, honey, or molasses, and maybe fat.

In America, *pancake* generally refers to the classic white-flour kind, often made with buttermilk. But this was not always so. The original American pancake was made from ground cornmeal by the Narraganset Native Americans, who called it *nokehick*. It was introduced to European settlers in the early 1600s, and its name was eventually corrupted into English as "no cake." (Imagine the confusion that might have been caused by a sign on the window of a roadside tavern at the time: "Yes, we have no cakes!")

In the 1700s, the Dutch added buckwheat *pannekoeken* to the American menu, and the British introduced the tradition of pancake feasts, held on Shrove Tuesday as a final binge before the deprivation of Lent. (Pre-Lenten pancake feasts and celebrations, which range from pancake-eating contests and flipping races to elaborate cooking competitions, live on in many parts of the world. The Sunday morning pancake breakfasts popular in churches throughout America are direct descendants of this tradition.)

By the 1800s, Americans had progressed from *no cakes* to *hoecakes*—thick cornmeal cakes so named because they were cooked on the blade of a hoe over an open fire by field laborers—and rice cakes made from milled rice flour. From Rhode Island came delicate cornmeal johnnycakes. Miners and lumberjacks in the Northwest favored sourdough pancakes made from a "wild" yeast starter. When provisions were in short supply, they invented thick and hearty flannel cakes—more colorfully known as "sweat pads"—made from stale bread soaked in milk.

With the current interest in regional American cooking, people are rediscovering all kinds of wonderful recipes and variations drawn from our collective pancake past. We've included several in this book. Many are made with a variety of healthful and tasty whole grains, along with a handful of basic ingredients you probably already have on hand. We hope you have fun trying them, and that they inspire you to create a few pancake traditions of your own.

## A Pancake by Any Other Name

Shakespeare himself recognized the appeal of a good pancake feed. Just listen to this irresistible invitation from *Pericles, Prince of Tyre* (Act 2, Scene 1):

"We'll have flesh for holidays, fish for fasting-days, and moreo'er puddings and flap-jacks, and thou shalt be welcome."

To which we reply, "If flap-jacks be the food of love, flip on."

# Bette's Diner Buttermilk Pancakes

*About 24 (4-inch) pancakes; serves 4*

Without a doubt, America's flapjack of choice is the good old buttermilk pancake, and at Bette's Diner, they're a perennial favorite. This is the recipe we've perfected over the years. It makes what we humbly consider to be the definitive pancake—sweet and cakey with a rich buttery flavor and appealing golden brown color.

> 2 cups all-purpose flour
> 2 tablespoons sugar
> 2 teaspoons baking powder
> 1 teaspoon baking soda
> $1/2$ teaspoon salt
> 2 eggs
> 2 cups buttermilk
> $1/2$ cup milk
> $1/4$ cup butter, melted

## Buttermilk Waffles

The buttermilk pancake recipe, without any modifications, makes wonderful waffles. For an extra light, crispy waffle, you can separate the eggs and beat the whites until they are stiff but not dry, then prepare the batter as directed, folding in the whites last.

In a large bowl, combine the flour, sugar, baking powder, baking soda, and salt. In a separate bowl, lightly beat the eggs, buttermilk, milk, and butter. Add the liquid ingredients to the dry ingredients all at once, stirring just to blend. The batter should be slightly lumpy and quite thick. Let the batter rest for 5 to 10 minutes.

Heat a lightly oiled griddle or heavy skillet over medium-high heat (375°F on an electric griddle). Portion $1/4$-cup measures of batter onto the hot griddle, spacing them apart. Cook for 2 to 3 minutes, until bubbles cover the surface of the pancakes, and their undersides are lightly browned. Gently turn them over and cook for about 2 minutes more, until the other sides are browned.

## VARIATIONS AND ADDITIONS

These work well with buttermilk pancakes and many of the other pancake recipes in this book.

- Bette's Blueberry Pancakes: *To the batter, add 1 cup fresh, thawed frozen, or drained canned blueberries, and 1/2 teaspoon freshly grated orange zest. If using fresh berries, dust them lightly with flour to keep them suspended in the batter and prevent their color from running. Sprinkle the finished pancakes with confectioners' sugar and serve with whipped butter and Citrus Maple Syrup (page 102) or Blueberry Compote Topping (page 103).*

- Darryl Kimble's Apple Pancakes: *To the batter, add 1 cup diced, peeled tart apple (about 1 large apple) tossed in 2 teaspoons sugar. Serve with Warm Apple-Currant Topping (page 104).*

- Butter Pecan Pancakes: *Melt 2 tablespoons butter in a heavy skillet over medium heat. Add 1/2 cup chopped pecans, 2 tablespoons sugar, and a few drops of lemon juice. Cook, stirring, for about 2 minutes, until the pecans are lightly toasted, and the sugar is just beginning to caramelize. Cool slightly and stir the mixture into the batter. Serve the pancakes with warm maple syrup and butter.*

> ## No Buttermilk? No Problem!
>
> You wake up craving fluffy buttermilk pancakes but don't feel like running to the store for buttermilk. If you've got plain yogurt, you're still in the game. Substitute 2 cups of yogurt for the buttermilk in this recipe. (If the batter looks too thick, add a little extra milk.) You might never make buttermilk pancakes with buttermilk again.

- Pigs in Blankets: *Roll pancakes around cooked breakfast sausage—either pork or chicken-apple—allowing three to four pancakes and links per serving. Dust with powdered sugar and serve with Warm Apple-Currant Topping (page 104).*

*(continued)*

- Banana Upside-Down Pancakes: *Slice three ripe bananas crosswise into 1/8- to 1/4-inch-thick disks; toss the banana slices with 2 tablespoons sugar. Grease the griddle well. For each pancake, place 4 or 5 banana slices directly on the griddle in a circle slightly smaller than your finished pancake will be; immediately pour 1/4 cup batter over the bananas to cover them. Cook as directed in the recipe. When you flip these pancakes, the sugared banana slices will be face-up and will have become deliciously and attractively caramelized.*

- Bacon Breakfast Cakes: *Cook 4 slices of bacon until crisp, then drain, crumble, and add to the batter. Serve the pancakes in stacks of two, topping each stack with a fried egg.*

- Strawberry Short Stack: *Toss 1 cup sliced strawberries with 1 tablespoon sugar. Place the strawberry slices on the surface of the half-cooked pancakes just before flipping. Sprinkle the finished pancakes with confectioners' sugar and serve with whipped cream and additional sliced strawberries.*

# Classic Griddle Cakes

*About 20 (3 1/2-inch) pancakes; serves 4*

You've probably got everything you need to make these basic pancakes in your kitchen right now. They're a bit less rich and fluffy than our buttermilk pancakes, but very satisfying all the same.

> 2 cups all-purpose flour
> 3 tablespoons sugar
> 1 tablespoon baking powder
> 1/2 teaspoon salt
> 2 eggs
> 1 1/2 cups milk
> 1/4 cup butter, melted

In a large bowl, combine the flour, sugar, baking powder, and salt. In a separate bowl, lightly beat the eggs, milk, and butter. Add the liquid ingredients to the dry ingredients all at once, stirring just to blend. The batter should be slightly lumpy. Let the batter rest for 5 to 10 minutes.

Heat a lightly oiled griddle or heavy skillet over medium-high heat (375°F on an electric griddle). Portion scant 1/4-cup measures of batter onto the hot griddle, spacing them apart. Cook for 2 to 3 minutes, until bubbles cover the surface of the pancakes, and their undersides are lightly browned. Gently turn them over and cook for about 2 minutes more, until the other sides are browned.

# Crunchy Whole-Wheat Walnut Hotcakes

*About 20 (4-inch) pancakes; serves 4*

A nod to our Berkeley roots, these are fluffier and more refined than most whole-grain hotcakes. Try them with yogurt and fresh fruit or Warm Apple-Currant Topping (page 104).

> 1 cup whole-wheat flour
> 1/2 cup all-purpose flour
> 6 tablespoons wheat germ
> 2 teaspoons baking powder
> 1 teaspoon baking soda
> 1/2 teaspoon salt
> 1/2 cup chopped walnuts
> 2 eggs
> 1 1/2 cups plain yogurt
> 1 cup milk
> 1/4 cup vegetable oil
> 3 tablespoons honey

In a large bowl, combine the whole-wheat flour, all-purpose flour, wheat germ, baking powder, baking soda, and salt; stir in the walnuts. In a separate bowl, lightly beat the eggs, yogurt, milk, oil, and honey. Add the liquid ingredients to the dry ingredients all at once, stirring just to blend. The batter should be slightly lumpy. Let the batter rest for 5 to 10 minutes.

Heat a lightly oiled griddle or heavy skillet over medium-high heat (375°F on an electric griddle). Portion 1/4-cup measures of batter onto the hot griddle, spacing them apart. Cook for 2 to 3 minutes, until bubbles cover the surface of the pancakes, and their undersides are lightly browned. Gently turn them over and cook for about 2 minutes more, until the other sides are browned.

# Oatmeal-Raisin Pancakes

*About 16 (4-inch) pancakes; serves 4*

Rolled oats give pancakes an appealingly toothsome texture.
We like these with chicken-apple breakfast sausages and
Warm Apple-Currant Topping (page 104).

> 1¹/₂ cups all-purpose or whole-wheat flour
> ¹/₂ cup quick-cooking rolled oats
> 3 tablespoons brown sugar
> 1 tablespoon baking powder
> ¹/₂ teaspoon salt
> 2 eggs
> 1¹/₂ cups milk
> ¹/₄ cup butter, melted
> ¹/₂ cup golden raisins
> ¹/₂ cup chopped walnuts (optional)

In a large bowl, combine the flour, oats, sugar, baking powder,
and salt. In a separate bowl, lightly beat the eggs, milk, and
butter. Add the liquid ingredients to the dry ingredients all at
once, stirring just to blend. Fold in the raisins and walnuts.
The batter should be slightly lumpy. Let the batter rest for 5 to
10 minutes.

Heat a lightly oiled griddle or heavy skillet over medium-
high heat (375°F on an electric griddle). Portion ¹/₄-cup measures of batter onto the hot griddle, spacing them apart. Cook
for 2 to 3 minute, until bubbles cover the surface of the pancakes, and their undersides are lightly browned. Gently turn
them over and cook for about 2 minutes more, until the other
sides are browned.

# Gingerbread Pancakes

*About 16 (4-inch) pancakes; serves 4*

These satisfying, not-too-sweet pancakes have been a popular wintertime special at the Diner since the early '90s. If you're deft with a ladle, try making "gingerbread man–cakes" right on the griddle—with currant eyes and buttons, of course.

> *1 cup whole-wheat flour*
> *1 cup all-purpose flour*
> *1 1/2 teaspoons baking soda*
> *1 teaspoon baking powder*
> *1 teaspoon ground ginger*
> *1 teaspoon ground cinnamon*
> *1/2 teaspoon ground cloves*
> *1/2 teaspoon salt*
> *1 cup hot, freshly brewed coffee*
> *1 cup sugar*
> *1/2 cup milk*
> *1/4 cup molasses*
> *1/2 cup butter, melted*
> *2 eggs, lightly beaten*

## FOR SERVING

*Confectioners' sugar*
*Whipped cream*
*Crystallized ginger, chopped (optional)*

In a large bowl, combine the whole-wheat flour, all-purpose flour, baking soda, baking powder, ground ginger, cinnamon, cloves, and salt. In a separate bowl, combine the coffee and sugar. Stir until the sugar is dissolved, then add the milk, molasses, butter, and eggs. Add the liquid ingredients to the dry ingredients all at once, stirring just to blend. The batter should be fairly thin and pourable. Let the batter rest for 5 to 10 minutes.

Heat a lightly oiled griddle or heavy skillet over medium-high heat (375°F on an electric griddle). Portion 1/4-cup measures of batter onto the hot griddle, spacing them apart. Cook for 3 to 4 minutes, until bubbles cover the surface of the pancakes, and their undersides are browned. Gently turn them over and cook for about 2 minutes more, until the other sides are browned.

Dust the pancakes with confectioners' sugar and top each serving with a dollop of whipped cream and a sprinkling of crystallized ginger.

## Baker's Bonus!

On a whim, we tried baking this batter and were delighted to discover that it makes a really outstanding gingerbread! Just pour the batter into a greased 8-inch-square baking pan and bake it at 350°F for about 25 minutes, or until a toothpick inserted in the center comes out clean.

# Spiced Pumpkin Pancakes

*About 16 (3 1/2-inch) pancakes; serves 4*

These show up on our menu every fall and tend to stick around all winter long. We make them with fresh pumpkin purée (we halve, lightly oil, and roast small Sugar Pie pumpkins in a 400°F oven until they're soft), but this easy version delivers great results with canned pumpkin. At the Diner, we like to serve them with homemade cranberry sauce, but they're every bit as tasty with Cranberries and Cream (page 106) or just with maple syrup.

> 1 1/4 cups all-purpose flour
> 2 teaspoons baking powder
> 1/2 teaspoon ground cinnamon
> 1/4 teaspoon ground allspice
> 1/4 teaspoon ground ginger
> 3/4 cup canned pumpkin
> 1 cup milk
> 2 eggs, separated
> 3 tablespoons dark brown sugar
> 2 tablespoons butter, melted
> 1/4 teaspoon salt
> Confectioners' sugar, for serving

In a large bowl, combine the flour, baking powder, cinnamon, allspice, and ginger. In a separate bowl, combine the pumpkin, milk, egg yolks, brown sugar, butter, and salt. Add the liquid ingredients to the dry ingredients all at once, stirring just to blend. The batter should be slightly lumpy. Place the egg whites in a separate bowl. With an electric mixer or whisk, beat until the whites are stiff but not dry. Gently fold the whites into the batter, just until combined.

Heat a lightly oiled griddle or heavy skillet over medium-high heat (375°F on an electric griddle). Portion scant 1/4-cup measures of batter onto the hot griddle, spacing them apart. Cook for 2 to 3 minutes, until bubbles cover the surface of the pancakes, and their undersides are lightly browned. Gently turn them over and cook for about 2 minutes more, until the other sides are browned. Dust the pancakes with confectioners' sugar just before serving.

# Souffléed Lemon–Poppy Seed Pancakes

*About 12 (3-inch) pancakes; serves 2 to 4*

Fluffy, tangy, and just right for a light, elegant brunch. For greatest enjoyment, make these on a spring morning, with sunlight pouring through the kitchen window.

*3 eggs, separated*
*1 cup whole-milk yogurt*
*3 tablespoons butter, melted*
*2 teaspoons freshly squeezed lemon juice*
*1 teaspoon grated lemon zest*
*¹/₂ cup all-purpose flour*
*3 tablespoons sugar*
*2 tablespoons poppy seeds*
*Pinch of salt*

## FOR SERVING

*Confectioners' sugar*
*Blueberry or strawberry preserves*

In a small bowl, beat the egg yolks with the yogurt, butter, lemon juice, and zest. In a large bowl, combine the flour, sugar, and poppy seeds. Add the liquid ingredients to the dry ingredients all at once, stirring just to blend. The batter should be slightly lumpy. Place the egg whites and salt in a separate bowl. With an electric mixer or whisk, beat until the whites are stiff but not dry. Gently fold the whites into the batter, just until combined.

Heat a lightly oiled griddle or heavy skillet over medium-high heat (375°F on an electric griddle). Portion the batter by heaping tablespoonfuls onto the hot griddle, spacing them apart. Cook for 2 to 3 minutes, until bubbles cover the surface of the pancakes, and their undersides are lightly browned. Gently turn them over and cook for 1 to 3 minutes more, until the other sides are browned. Dust the pancakes with confectioners' sugar and pass the preserves at the table.

# Double-Chocolate Devil's Food Pancakes

*About 16 (4-inch) pancakes; serves 4*

Life is short. Eat dessert for breakfast. These rich, dark chocolate–chocolate chip pancakes make a fine choice for a special occasion—like Valentine's Day (dig out those heart-shaped pancake molds), Mother's Day, Father's Day, or a chocolate lover's birthday. They also make a memorable dessert, especially when served with ice cream and warm chocolate sauce. For added drama, dust the plate with cocoa powder.

*2 cups all-purpose flour*
*1 cup sugar*
*1 teaspoon baking soda*
*1 teaspoon baking powder*
*1/2 teaspoon salt*
*1 cup hot, freshly brewed coffee*
*1/2 cup unsweetened cocoa powder (preferably
    Dutch-processed)*
*1/2 cup milk*
*1/2 cup butter, melted*
*2 eggs*
*1 teaspoon pure vanilla extract*
*1 cup mini semisweet chocolate chips*

## FOR SERVING

*Confectioners' sugar*
*Whipped cream*
*Chocolate sauce, warm (optional)*

In a large bowl, combine the flour, sugar, baking soda, baking powder, and salt. In a separate bowl, combine the coffee and cocoa. Whisk until the cocoa is dissolved, then add the milk and butter. Lightly beat in the eggs and vanilla. Add the liquid ingredients to the dry ingredients all at once, stirring just to blend. Fold in the chocolate chips. The batter should be slightly lumpy. Let the batter rest for 5 to 10 minutes.

*(continued)*

Heat a lightly oiled griddle or heavy skillet over medium-high heat (375°F on an electric griddle). Portion 1/4-cup measures of batter onto the hot griddle, spacing them apart. Cook for 2 to 3 minutes, until bubbles cover the surface of the pancakes, and their undersides are browned. Gently turn them over and cook for about 2 minutes more, until the other sides are browned.

Dust the pancakes with confectioners' sugar and top each serving with a dollop of whipped cream. Lily-gilders: pass warm chocolate sauce at the table.

# Jane Lindeman's Blueberry Yogurt Pancakes

*About 24 (4-inch) pancakes; serves 4*

Everyone knows adding blueberries to pancakes is a sure bet. Our friend Jane thought of a way to up the ante: adding blueberry yogurt. These extra-moist cakes greet you with a hit of super blueberry aroma even before you bite in. The recipe works best with high-quality, whole-milk yogurt, preferably the kind with whole fruit at the bottom. You can also use raspberry or strawberry yogurt with raspberries or sliced strawberries.

>  *2 cups all-purpose flour*
>  *2 tablespoons sugar*
>  *2 teaspoons baking powder*
>  *1 teaspoon baking soda*
>  *1/2 teaspoon salt*
>  *2 eggs*
>  *11/2 cups (12 ounces) blueberry yogurt*
>  *3/4 cup milk*
>  *1/4 cup butter, melted*
>  *1/2 teaspoon finely grated lemon zest*
>  *1 cup fresh blueberries, lightly dusted with flour*

In a large bowl, combine the flour, sugar, baking powder, baking soda, and salt. In a separate bowl, lightly beat the eggs, yogurt, milk, butter, and lemon zest. Add the liquid ingredients to the dry ingredients all at once, stirring just to blend. Fold in the blueberries. The batter should be slightly lumpy. Let the batter rest for 5 to 10 minutes.

Heat a lightly oiled griddle or heavy skillet over medium-high heat (375°F on an electric griddle). Portion 1/4-cup measures of batter onto the hot griddle, spacing them apart. Cook for 2 to 3 minutes, until bubbles cover the surface of the pancakes, and their undersides are lightly browned. Gently turn them over and cook for about 2 minutes more, until the other sides are browned.

# Cornmeal—It's All in the Grind

There's no food more American than corn. And cornmeal pancakes—with their winning combination of delicate, crunchy texture and sweet, substantial flavor—have evolved as a uniquely American specialty.

Cornmeal, ground from dried corn kernels, comes in three textures: fine, medium, and coarse. For pancakes, which cook quickly, fine cornmeal is the way to go. Save the coarse-ground stuff for polenta or for use as a breading.

Cornmeal is also available in three colors—yellow, white, and blue—depending on the type of corn from which it was made. At Bette's, we generally use yellow cornmeal. It tends to be more flavorful than white cornmeal, and we like the bright color it brings to the plate.

All cornmeal is not created equal. At the Diner, we use stone-ground (sometimes called water-ground) cornmeal. It's milled between water-powered stone grinding wheels, a process that preserves some of the hull and germ of the corn. The result is a nutritious product with a rich, nutty, whole-grain flavor. Most major commercial brands of cornmeal, on the other hand, are steel-cut. This process strips away almost all of the germ and husk, breaks down the natural fiber of the corn, and reduces its nutritional value and flavor.

Stone-ground cornmeal can be found in health food stores and some supermarkets. It's worth tracking down. Because it contains some fat from the germ, it's more perishable than the steel-ground variety. Buy it in bulk from a store with high turnover and check to be sure there are no stale or rancid odors when you lift the lid of the bin. Store stone-ground cornmeal in the refrigerator for up to four months, or, better yet, buy just what you need for a recipe or two.

# Golden Cornmeal Pancakes

*About 18 (3¹/₂-inch) pancakes; serves 4*

These pancakes are the star attraction of our Virginia Breakfast: three corn cakes, a grilled smoked pork chop, and custardy scrambled eggs. They're light and sweet with a tender crunch. We also like them blini style, topped with crème fraîche and smoked salmon, trout, or sturgeon. Cake flour makes them extra fluffy, but if you don't have it on hand, you can use all-purpose flour.

2 cups water
1/4 cup butter, plus more for serving
2 cups fine yellow cornmeal
1¹/₂ teaspoons salt
2 tablespoons sugar
2 eggs
1 cup milk
1 cup cake flour
4 teaspoons baking powder
Warm maple syrup, for serving

## Fresh Corn Pancakes

Add ¹/₂ cup uncooked, freshly shucked sweet corn kernels to the batter and cook as directed.

In a small saucepan over high heat, bring the water and butter to a rolling boil. In a large bowl, combine the cornmeal, salt, and sugar. Pour the boiling water and butter over the cornmeal mixture and stir to combine. Cover the bowl with plastic wrap or a clean kitchen towel and let it rest for 10 minutes, until the liquid is absorbed and the cornmeal has the texture of a thick mush.

In a separate bowl, beat together the eggs and milk. Add the flour and baking powder and mix lightly. Add the egg mixture to the cornmeal mixture, stirring gently just to combine. The batter should be thick and slightly lumpy.

Heat a lightly oiled griddle or heavy skillet over medium-high heat (375°F on an electric griddle). Portion scant ¹/₄-cup measures of batter onto the hot griddle, spacing them apart.

*(continued)*

Cook for 2 to 3 minutes, until bubbles cover the surface of the pancakes, and their undersides are lightly browned. Gently turn them over and cook for about 2 minutes more, until the other sides are browned. Serve immediately with butter and warm maple syrup.

## Cornmeal Waffles

The cornmeal pancake recipe, without any modifications, makes outstanding waffles that are the ultimate complement to fried chicken. For an extra-light, crispy waffle, you can separate the eggs and beat the whites with an electric mixer or whisk until they are stiff but not dry. Then prepare the batter as directed, beating the yolks with the milk and folding in the whites last. (You can add $1/2$ cup uncooked, fresh corn kernels to this batter too.) Pour $1/2$ to $3/4$ cup of batter (check the manufacturer's directions) onto the hot waffle iron, close the lid, and bake the waffle until it stops steaming and is nicely browned.

# Quick Cornmeal Pancakes with Dried Cherries

*About 16 (3 1/2-inch) pancakes; serves 4*

These delicate pancakes can be made in short order because there's no need to pre-cook the cornmeal. The dried cherries moisten as they cook and taste wonderful with the cornmeal. Currants, raisins, dried cranberries, and chopped dried apricots work well too. If you don't have buttermilk, substitute plain yogurt.

> 1 cup all-purpose flour
> 1/2 cup fine yellow cornmeal
> 3 tablespoons sugar
> 2 teaspoons baking powder
> 1 teaspoon baking soda
> 1/8 teaspoon salt
> 1/3 cup coarsely chopped dried cherries
> 2 eggs
> 1 1/4 cups buttermilk
> 1/4 cup butter, melted

In a large bowl, combine the flour, cornmeal, sugar, baking powder, baking soda, and salt. Stir in the cherries. In a separate bowl, lightly beat the eggs and stir in the buttermilk and butter. Add the liquid ingredients to the dry ingredients all at once, stirring just to blend. The batter should be thick and slightly lumpy.

Heat a lightly oiled griddle or heavy skillet over medium-high heat (375°F on an electric griddle). Portion scant 1/4-cup measures of batter onto the hot griddle, spacing them apart. Cook for 2 to 3 minutes, until bubbles cover the surface of the pancakes, and their undersides are lightly browned. Gently turn them over and cook for about 2 minutes more, until the other sides are browned.

# Lacy Johnny Cakes

*About 32 (3-inch) pancakes; serves 4*

Cornmeal pancakes got their start in the South as hoecakes (originally cooked right on the blade of a hoe over an open fire) and corn pone—both eggless quick breads made by frying or baking patties of cornmeal mush. Corn cakes headed north in the early 1700s, when Rhode Islanders began using heart-shaped cast-iron griddles heated over the hot coals of an open fire to cook thick cornmeal patties called johnny cakes. Pancake scholars continue to debate the origins of this name. It may have come from "journey cakes" (the hearty cakes were great road food), "Shawnee cakes," or even a corruption of the Dutch, *pannekoeken*. In any event, Rhode Islanders take the matter seriously. The use of white or yellow cornmeal, eggs, water, and scalded milk are all hotly contested, and there's even a Society for the Preservation of Johnnycake Tradition. Two warring camps have arisen: one side spells "Johnny" with the "h," the other without—a debate that has reached the floor of the state legislature. But then, Rhode Islanders call milk shakes "cabinets," so their language appears to have a logic of its own.

We've invented our own version. The batter is thinner than most, and the pancakes spread quickly on the griddle. You'll see why we call them "lacy." As they cook, they become covered with tiny bubbles. These pancakes cook quickly, so be prepared to stand by the stove. They're delicious on their own with maple or fruit syrup, or served with ham and eggs.

> *2 cups milk*
> *1 cup fine yellow cornmeal*
> *6 tablespoons butter, melted*
> *2 tablespoons sugar*
> *1/2 teaspoon salt*
> *2 eggs, lightly beaten*

In a small saucepan, scald the milk by heating it over medium-high heat to just below the boiling point. Remove from the heat.

Place the cornmeal in a bowl and pour in the scalded milk. Stir lightly to combine. Cover the bowl with plastic wrap or a clean kitchen towel and let it rest for 10 minutes. Stir in the butter, sugar, salt, and eggs. The batter should be thin and pourable.

Heat a liberally oiled griddle or heavy skillet over medium-high heat (375°F on an electric griddle). Pour the batter by tablespoonfuls onto the griddle. The batter will spread quickly and should sizzle immediately, forming tiny bubbles (if it doesn't, turn up the heat). Cook the pancakes for 30 seconds, until their undersides are nicely browned. Gently turn them over and cook for 30 seconds more, until the other sides are lightly browned.

# More Bang for
# Your Buckwheat

Despite its name, buckwheat bears no relation to wheat. In fact, even though it's cooked as a cereal and ground to make flour, buckwheat is actually not a grain at all, but a wild herb—a distant cousin of rhubarb—native to Russia and Central Asia. It was introduced to the West in the Middle Ages by Dutch traders who are believed to have named it *boek weit,* or "book wheat," a reference to the Bible. Buckwheat caught on in Europe because it is practically indestructible and can be grown even in poor soil with little effort. Amateur farmers were once known as buckwheaters.

The seeds of the buckwheat plant are ground to make buckwheat flour or are hulled and crushed to make groats, also known as kasha. Buckwheat flour is of little value in bread baking because it lacks gluten, but it does make outstanding pancakes with a distinctive tangy flavor. In fact, it's thought of primarily as a pancake flour by cooks all over the world, and turns up in everything from Russian blini to the galettes of Brittany.

Buckwheat is a naturally healthy food. Because it's a hearty plant, it has traditionally been grown organically without pesticides. It's also the best-known source of complex carbohydrates and is nearly a complete protein, offering more than 80 percent of the protein of eggs with no cholesterol or fat. And it's ideal for people on wheat-free diets.

Buckwheat flour isn't usually used alone in pancakes, because that would make them too thick and heavy. But use it in combination with wheat flour and beaten egg whites, yeast, or other leavening agents, and you'll find it produces a wonderfully soft, silky batter and tender, nutty pancakes that rise delicately from the griddle.

# Fluffy Buckwheat Pancakes

*About 12 (4-inch) pancakes; serves 2 to 4*

Buckwheat cakes are a weekly special at the Diner. We serve them with pepper-cured bacon, eggs any style, butter, and a pitcher of Vermont maple syrup. They're also delicious with fresh fruit and yogurt.

If you're having trouble finding a store that carries buckwheat flour, or you don't want to keep buttermilk on hand, you can save a step and buy a bag of Bette's Diner Buckwheat Pancake and Waffle Mix. But if you've got the time and the ingredients, here's the secret formula.

*1/2 cup all-purpose flour*
*1/2 cup buckwheat flour*
*1 1/2 teaspoons baking powder*
*1/2 teaspoon baking soda*
*1 1/2 teaspoons sugar*
*1/2 teaspoon salt*
*1 egg, separated*
*1 cup buttermilk*
*1/4 cup water*
*2 tablespoons butter, melted*

## Buckwheat Waffles

Without any modifications, our buckwheat pancake recipe makes outstanding waffles. Pour 1/2 to 3/4 cup of batter (check the manufacturer's directions) onto the hot waffle iron, close the lid and bake the waffle until it stops steaming and is nicely browned. Serve with fruit syrup, maple syrup, or fruit and yogurt.

In a large bowl, combine the all-purpose flour, buckwheat flour, baking powder, baking soda, sugar, and salt. In a separate bowl, combine the egg yolk, buttermilk, water, and butter. Add the liquid ingredients to the dry ingredients all at once, stirring just to blend. In a small bowl, beat the egg white with a whisk until it forms soft peaks. Gently fold the egg white into the batter.

Heat a lightly oiled griddle or heavy skillet over medium-high heat (375°F on an electric griddle). Portion 1/4-cup measures of batter onto the hot griddle, spacing them apart. Cook for 2 to 3 minutes, until bubbles cover the surface of the pancakes, and their undersides are lightly browned. Gently turn them over and cook for about 2 minutes more, until the other sides are browned.

# Blini

*About 48 (2¹/₂-inch) pancakes; serves 4*

When we cater parties, we often serve our Fluffy Buckwheat
Pancakes (page 45) as a fancy finger food. We make them the
size of silver dollars and top them with sour cream and caviar
or smoked salmon—our version of blini, the famous Russian
buckwheat pancakes. Real blini are a bit more complex because
they're made with yeast, which gives them a slightly sour flavor
and an addictively light texture. They're worth the effort.

> ³/₄ cup all-purpose flour
> ³/₄ cup buckwheat flour
> 1 envelope (2¹/₄ teaspoons) active dry yeast
> 2 tablespoons sugar
> ¹/₄ teaspoon salt
> 1¹/₂ cups milk
> ¹/₄ cup butter, cut into small pieces
> 2 eggs, lightly beaten

## FOR SERVING

> ¹/₄ cup butter, melted
> ¹/₂ cup crème fraîche or sour cream
> 2 ounces caviar, or ¹/₂ pound smoked salmon, trout, or
>     whitefish, thinly sliced or flaked

In a large bowl, combine the all-purpose flour, buckwheat
flour, yeast, sugar, and salt.

In a small, heavy saucepan, combine the milk and butter
over low heat. Heat until just warm, not hot (105° to 115°F),
and the butter has melted.

Stir the milk mixture into the flour mixture. Stir in the
eggs. Using an electric mixer on low speed, beat for about
1 minute until smooth, or beat vigorously by hand for 3 to
5 minutes until smooth. Cover the bowl and set it in a warm
place for 1 to 1¹/₂ hours, until the batter is doubled in volume
and light and bubbly. At this point, the batter can be used

immediately or refrigerated for up to 8 hours (bring to room temperature before proceeding).

Heat a lightly oiled griddle or heavy skillet over medium-high heat (375°F on an electric griddle). Stir down the batter. Portion the batter by tablespoonfuls onto the hot griddle, spacing them apart. Cook for 2 to 3 minutes, until bubbles cover the surface of the pancakes, and their undersides are lightly browned. Gently turn them over and cook for about 2 minutes more, until the other sides are browned.

Drizzle the pancakes with melted butter and top each with a dollop of crème fraîche and a little caviar.

## Don't Say "Pass Me a Blini"

Share this bit of trivia while indulging in blini with friends: The singular of *blini* is *blin*.

## Wild about Sourdough

In the evolution of bread baking, sourdough pancakes are the link between ancient unleavened flatbreads and modern yeasted breads. More than five thousand years ago, some unsuspecting Egyptian baker discovered that flour and water, left out in the open air overnight, began to froth and bubble, and that breads baked from this dough rose higher and had a lighter texture than unleavened breads. What this lucky baker had hit upon was the process of using "wild" airborne yeast—which converts starches and sugars into carbon dioxide gas—as a leavening agent.

Bakers eventually learned that the sour mixture could be kept alive indefinitely by "feeding" it more flour and water, so that a small bit of this starter could be used to leaven more bread. And from that time until the introduction of commercial powdered yeast in the nineteenth century, yeast starters or sponges were the leavening agents used in bread baking.

Today, some starters are alleged to be centuries old, and are highly prized for their distinctive flavor. Others—like the world-famous sourdough of San Francisco—are thought to benefit from a strain of special airborne yeast unique to the area.

That yeast adds something special to our fluffy sourdough pancakes and waffles across the Bay at the Diner too. When we decided to put them on our menu as a regular weekly pancake special, we borrowed a bit of "mother sponge" from Steve and Susie Sullivan at Berkeley's famous Acme Bakery up the street, and we've been using this same wonderful starter for years.

# Quick Sourdough Starter

*Makes 2 cups*

If you don't already happen to have a sourdough sponge made from airborne yeast on hand—and these days, who does?—here's a simple way to make sourdough starter from scratch using active dry yeast.

> *1 cup warm water (about 90°F)*
> *1 envelope (2¹/₄ teaspoons) active dry yeast*
> *1 cup all-purpose flour*

In a bowl, combine the water and yeast. Whisk in the flour, leaving the mixture slightly lumpy. Cover the bowl and let it sit in a warm place, between 70° and 75°F, for 8 hours, or until it begins to bubble and smell slightly sour. You should have about 2 cups of starter.

Your starter is now ready to use, or you can cover and refrigerate it for up to 2 weeks.

After 2 weeks, the starter will become rancid unless it is replenished. To replenish it, simply make a batch of sourdough pancakes as directed in the following recipe (in which half the starter is used and the other half replenished); or discard half the starter and add 1 cup milk and 1 cup flour to the remainder. As long as you continue replenishing half the starter at least every 2 weeks, it will last indefinitely.

Before replenishing or using a starter, always bring it to room temperature. If it develops a pinkish color or a strong, acrid aroma, discard it.

# San Francisco Sourdough Pancakes

*About 24 (4-inch) pancakes; serves 4*

These are delicious with maple syrup and a side of ham and eggs. Note that the starter needs time to compose itself—about eight hours or, perhaps more conveniently, overnight—before it can be used in a recipe.

## Sourdough Waffles

Without any modifications, the sourdough pancake recipe makes outstanding waffles. For an extra-light, crispy waffle, you can separate the eggs and beat the whites with an electric mixer or whisk until they are stiff but not dry, then prepare the batter as directed, folding in the whites last. Pour 1/2 to 3/4 cup of batter (check the manufacturer's directions) onto the hot waffle iron, close the lid, and bake the waffle until it stops steaming and is nicely browned.

*2 cups sourdough starter, at room temperature (page 49)*
*2 cups milk*
*2 cups all-purpose flour*
*2 eggs, beaten*
*2 tablespoons sugar*
*2 teaspoons baking soda*
*1/2 teaspoon salt*
*2 tablespoons butter, melted*

The night before cooking the pancakes, combine the starter with the milk and flour in a bowl. Place half of this mixture in a separate bowl, cover it with plastic wrap, and return it to the refrigerator. This is your replenished starter, which will last up to 2 weeks.

Loosely cover the bowl of starter-flour mixture (covering the bowl with a plate or towel works well) and set in a warm place, between 70° and 75°F, for at least 8 hours or overnight. The mixture will be bubbly and somewhat expanded in size, though not doubled in volume.

In the morning, add the eggs, sugar, baking soda, salt, and butter to the bowl and stir well. The batter will be thick and somewhat elastic. Let the batter rest for about 10 minutes.

Heat a lightly oiled griddle or heavy skillet over medium-high heat (375°F on an electric griddle). Portion 1/4-cup measures of batter onto the hot griddle, spacing them apart. Cook for 2 to 3 minutes, until bubbles cover the surface of the pancakes, and their undersides are lightly browned. Gently turn them over and cook for about 2 minutes more, until the other sides are browned.

# English Muffins

The English muffin is really the American cousin of the British crumpet. Both are related to the pancake because they are baked on a flat griddle. Crumpet batter is thin and liquid, and must be baked in crumpet rings—small metal ring molds that keep the batter from spreading on the griddle. English muffins are made from a stiffer dough that is kneaded to develop the gluten in the flour and then cut into rounds. The result is an airy pancake-bread filled with tiny cavities for butter and jam to lodge in. Our English muffins, leavened with sourdough starter, have a slightly tangy flavor and a delicate crumb.

> *1/2 cup sourdough starter, at room temperature (page 49)*
> *3 cups all-purpose flour*
> *1 cup milk*
> *2 tablespoons sugar*
> *1/2 teaspoon baking soda*
> *1/2 teaspoon salt*
> *Fine yellow cornmeal, for dusting*
> *Butter and jam, for serving*

In a large bowl, combine the starter, 2 cups of the flour, and the milk. Cover the bowl loosely and let it sit in a warm place, between 70° and 75°F, for at least 8 hours or overnight.

Add the sugar, baking soda, and salt to the bowl, stirring vigorously until the ingredients are well combined. The batter will be thick and somewhat elastic. Turn the dough out onto a well-floured surface and knead lightly for 3 to 5 minutes, adding up to 1 cup of the remaining flour a few tablespoons at a time, until the dough loses its stickiness.

On a well-floured surface, roll out the dough to 3/4 inch thick. Cut out circles with a 3-inch cookie cutter (or with the open end of a large tuna can). Lightly sprinkle both sides of each dough circle with cornmeal, and place the circles on an ungreased baking sheet, spaced 1 to 2 inches apart. Cover with a clean kitchen towel and set in a warm place for 1 hour, or until the dough doubles in volume.

Heat a lightly oiled griddle or heavy skillet over medium-high heat (375°F on an electric griddle). Cook the muffins for about 5 minutes on each side, until browned and cooked through. Like pancakes, English muffins should be turned only once.

Cool the muffins on a wire rack. Split them with a fork, toast them, and serve them with butter and jam.

# Low-Fat Pancakes

*About 16 (4-inch) pancakes; serves 4*

These are surprisingly tasty when smothered with maple syrup and served with a big dollop of whipped butter. Just kidding. Top them with warm applesauce and you'll find you *can* have your pancake and eat it too.

> 2 cups all-purpose flour
> 3 tablespoons sugar
> 1 tablespoon baking powder
> $1/2$ teaspoon salt
> 2 eggs
> $1^{1}/2$ cups skim milk
> $1/2$ cup applesauce, plus more for serving

In a large bowl, combine the flour, sugar, baking powder, and salt. In a separate bowl, lightly beat the eggs, milk, and applesauce. Add the liquid ingredients to the dry ingredients all at once, stirring just to blend. The batter should be slightly lumpy. Let the batter rest for 5 to 10 minutes.

Heat a lightly oiled griddle or heavy skillet over medium-high heat (375°F on an electric griddle). Portion 1/4-cup measures of batter onto the hot griddle, spacing them apart. Cook for 2 to 3 minutes, until bubbles cover the surface of the pancakes, and their undersides are lightly browned. Gently turn them over and cook for about 2 minutes more, until the other sides are browned.

Serve with warm applesauce.

# Quick Pantry Pancakes

*About 12 (3-inch) pancakes; serves 2 to 4*

These light pancakes from our friend Helen Gustafson are the fastest and simplest to prepare in this book. You can turn them out in about ten minutes, start to finish. Served with jam, fruit preserves, fresh berries, or other fruit, they make a simple, satisfying breakfast.

> *4 eggs*
> *1 cup cottage cheese*
> *2 tablespoons vegetable oil*
> *1/2 cup quick-cooking oats*
> *1/2 teaspoon baking soda*
> *1/4 teaspoon salt*

Combine the eggs, cottage cheese, oil, oats, baking soda, and salt, in that order, in a blender or food processor. Blend at top speed for 5 to 6 seconds. The batter should be thick and somewhat lumpy.

Heat a lightly oiled griddle or heavy skillet over medium-high heat (375°F on an electric griddle). Portion the batter by heaping tablespoonfuls onto the hot griddle, spacing them apart. Cook for 2 to 3 minutes, until bubbles cover the surface of the pancakes, and their undersides are lightly browned. Gently turn them over and cook for about 2 minutes more, until the other sides are browned.

# Dairy Pancakes

W e're using the term *dairy* here in the Yiddish sense, the way the Jewish dairy restaurants of New York's Lower East Side do. *Dairy* (or in Yiddish, *milchik*) simply refers to kosher meatless dishes (as opposed to *flaishik* dishes made with meat). Jewish dairy dishes aren't necessarily made with dairy products, though the holy trinity of sour cream, cottage cheese, and cream cheese tends to figure prominently.

The great dairy restaurants of New York, like Ratner's on Delancey Street, have contributed much to the American menu, especially when it comes breakfast and brunch foods—from bagels and lox to blintzes, matzo *brei*, potato latkes, cream herring, and knishes.

The pancakes served at these restaurants are of the Eastern European variety. At their finest, they are rich and flavorful, but also delicate and airy because they're often made with beaten egg whites and very little flour. Sour cream and fruit preserves are the classic accompaniments.

# Cottage Cheese Pancakes

*12 to 16 (3-inch) pancakes; serves 2 to 4*

After chicken soup, we think these simple pancakes are the original Jewish comfort food. Serve them with plenty of sour cream and jam.

*3 eggs, separated*
*3/4 cup large-curd cottage cheese*
*1/4 cup all-purpose flour*
*1/4 teaspoon salt*
*Sour cream and jam, for serving*

In a large bowl, beat the egg yolks until thick and pale. Stir in the cottage cheese. Add the flour and salt, stirring just to combine. Place the egg whites in a separate bowl. With an electric mixer or whisk, beat until the whites are stiff but not dry. Gently fold the whites into the yolk mixture, just until combined.

Heat a lightly oiled griddle or heavy skillet over medium-high heat (375°F on an electric griddle). Portion the batter by heaping table-spoonfuls onto the hot griddle, spacing them apart. Cook for about 2 minutes, until bubbles cover the surface of the pan-cakes, and their undersides are lightly browned. Gently turn them over and cook for about 2 minutes more, until the other sides are browned. Serve with sour cream and jam.

## Egg Whites

A rule of thumb for beating egg whites: Their stiffness should correspond to the consistency of the ingredients into which you will fold them. A heavy cake batter, for example, needs stiffer egg whites than a light, liquid pancake batter does.

# Fresh Breakfast Cheeses

Cottage cheese, sour cream, and cream cheese are supermarket staples, and we've all grown accustomed to their flavors and to the way they perform in cooking. But these days, there are fresher, better alternatives, thanks to a remarkable revival of local fresh cheese making throughout the United States.

Compared to factory-made cheese, artisan and farmstead cheeses are a revelation. An artisan cheese is made in small batches, mostly by hand, by people who care about quality and flavor, and about the relationship of their ingredients and products to the places where they live and work. A farmstead cheese is an artisan cheese made right on the dairy farm where the milk is produced. Like anything that's not mass-produced, these cheeses may be a bit more expensive, but their fresh flavors, creamy textures, and natural, wholesome ingredients make them well worth the extra cost.

At the diner, we buy our fresh cheeses from our founding partner Sue Conley, who, along with Peg Smith, created Cowgirl Creamery a few miles from Point Reyes National Seashore in Marin County. The Cowgirls use organic milk from the Straus Family Creamery down the road to make their fresh cheeses.

Wherever you live, we encourage you to seek out locally made fresh cheeses for pancake making and everyday enjoyment. Instead of that familiar tub of cottage cheese, look for one that's made by a small local dairy or try quark, a tart, yogurt-style cheese. In place of factory-made cream cheese, try farmer cheese or *fromage blanc*. This staple of the French diet, made with whole milk instead of cream, contains roughly 30 percent less fat than most cream cheese and about 80 percent more flavor. And instead of mass-market sour cream, consider substituting a locally produced, stabilizer-free crème fraîche. Try any of these products just once and you'll see what we mean: bringing home beautifully crafted ingredients like these will bring out the artisan pancake maker in you.

# Sour Cream Cloud Cakes

*About 24 (3-inch) pancakes; serves 4*

These are some of the lightest pancakes we've ever tasted, and they're remarkably easy to make. Just five ingredients, three steps, and they're all yours. Serve them with maple syrup or berry preserves.

*4 eggs*
*2 cups sour cream*
*2/3 cup all-purpose flour*
*2 teaspoons baking powder*
*1/4 teaspoon salt*

In a bowl, beat the eggs lightly. Blend in the sour cream. In a separate bowl, combine the flour, baking powder, and salt. Add the liquid ingredients to the dry ingredients, stirring just to combine. The batter should be very light and fluffy.

Heat a lightly oiled griddle or heavy skillet over medium-high heat (375°F on an electric griddle). Portion the batter by heaping tablespoonfuls onto the hot griddle, spacing them apart. Cook for 2 to 3 minutes, until bubbles cover the surface of the pancakes, and their undersides are lightly browned. Gently turn them over and cook for 1 to 2 minutes more, until the other sides are browned.

# Bananas-and-Sour-Cream Pancakes

*About 24 (4-inch) pancakes; serves 4*

If, like some of us, you had the good fortune to grow up eating an occasional Sunday morning bowlful of sliced bananas topped with a generous blob of sour cream, you'll have no trouble imagining how well this perfect combination translates to pancakes.

> *2 cups all-purpose flour*
> *2 tablespoons brown sugar*
> *2 teaspoons baking powder*
> *1 teaspoon baking soda*
> *1/2 teaspoon salt*
> *2 eggs*
> *1 cup sour cream*
> *1 1/2 cups milk*
> *1/4 cup butter, melted*
> *2 ripe bananas, 1 thinly sliced, 1 mashed*
> *1/2 cup chopped walnuts (optional)*

In a large bowl, combine the flour, sugar, baking powder, baking soda, and salt. In a separate bowl, lightly beat the eggs, sour cream, milk, and butter. Add the liquid ingredients to the dry ingredients all at once. Add the sliced and mashed bananas and walnuts, stirring just to blend. The batter should be slightly lumpy and quite thick. Let the batter rest for 5 to 10 minutes.

Heat a lightly oiled griddle or heavy skillet over medium-high heat (375°F on an electric griddle). Portion 1/4-cup measures of batter onto the hot griddle, spacing them apart. Cook for 2 to 3 minutes, until bubbles cover the surface of the pancakes, and their undersides are lightly browned. Gently turn them over and cook for about 2 minutes more, until the other sides are browned.

# Matzo Meal Pancakes

*12 to 16 (3-inch) pancakes; serves 2 to 4*

Matzo meal is nothing more than finely ground matzo, the thin, unleavened cracker bread served during the Passover holiday. It's used in matzo balls and gefilte fish, and it makes delicious, fluffy pancakes. You can find matzo meal in the specialty or Jewish foods section of most large supermarkets.

*3 eggs, separated*
*1/2 cup matzo meal*
*1/2 cup water*
*1/2 teaspoon salt*
*1/2 teaspoon sugar*

In a large bowl, beat the egg yolks lightly. Add the matzo meal, water, salt, and sugar, and stir to combine. Place the egg whites in a separate bowl. With an electric mixer or whisk, beat until the whites are stiff but not dry. Gently fold the whites into the yolk mixture, just until combined

Heat a lightly oiled griddle or heavy skillet over medium-high heat (375°F on an electric griddle). Portion the batter by heaping tablespoonfuls onto the hot griddle, spacing them apart. Cook for about 2 minutes, until bubbles cover the surface of the pancakes, and their undersides are lightly browned. Gently turn them over and cook for 1 to 2 minutes more, until the other sides are browned.

# Golda Meir's Matzo Brei

*Serves 2 to 4*

Golda Meir, the prime minister of Israel from 1969 to 1974, was also, for a time, Bette's great-aunt by marriage. On a trip to Israel in 1971, Bette spent a memorable five days at Golda's place in Jerusalem. She remembers sitting at the kitchen table, talking about life and politics, while the P.M. chain-smoked Pall Malls. One morning, Golda prepared matzo *brei*—the best Bette had ever tasted. This is how she made it, and how we make it at the Diner.

We serve Golda's matzo *brei* with a generous dollop of sour cream on the side, but some prefer it with jam or applesauce.

> *3 eggs*
> *1/2 teaspoon salt*
> *4 matzos*
> *2 cups boiling water*
> *2 tablespoons butter*
> *Sour cream, berry jam, or applesauce, for serving*

Beat the eggs well in a large bowl. Add the salt. In a separate bowl, crumble the matzos into 1-inch pieces. Pour the boiling water over the crumbled matzos, soak for about 30 seconds, then drain the matzos in a colander set in the sink. Add the drained matzos to the beaten eggs, stirring to combine well.

In a 10-inch nonstick pan, melt the butter over medium-high heat. Add the matzo mixture, spreading it evenly across the bottom of the pan. Fry for 3 to 4 minutes, until the underside is golden brown and the mixture has formed a fairly solid mass. Flip the matzo *brei* in one piece by covering the pan with a plate, inverting the matzo *brei* onto the plate and sliding it back into the pan. Cook the other side for 3 to 4 minutes more, until it is nicely browned, the egg is just set, and the entire matzo *brei* is cooked through. Cut into wedges and serve with sour cream, jam, or applesauce.

# Rice and Sesame Pancakes

*About 16 (4-inch) pancakes; serves 4*

Cooked rice and crunchy sesame seeds give these pancakes
an appealing texture and a soothing flavor reminiscent of rice
pudding. This is a good way to use up leftover cooked rice.

> 1 1/2 cups all-purpose flour
> 1 tablespoon baking powder
> 1 1/2 teaspoons sugar
> 1/2 teaspoon salt
> 2 eggs, separated
> 2 cups milk
> 1/4 cup butter, melted
> 1 teaspoon pure vanilla extract
> 1/8 teaspoon pure almond extract (optional)
> 1/2 cup cooked rice, at room temperature
> 2 tablespoons toasted sesame seeds
> Maple syrup, sour cream, or berry jam, for serving

In a large bowl, combine the flour, baking powder, sugar, and
salt. In a separate bowl, combine the egg yolks, milk, butter,
vanilla extract, and almond extract. Add the liquid ingredients
to the dry ingredients all at once, stirring just to blend. Fold in
the rice and sesame seeds. Place the egg whites in a separate
bowl. With an electric mixer or whisk, beat until the whites
are stiff but not dry. Gently fold the whites into the batter, just
until combined.

Heat a lightly oiled griddle or heavy skillet over medium-
high heat (375°F on an electric griddle). Portion 1/4-cup measures of batter onto the hot griddle, spacing them apart. Cook
for 2 to 3 minutes, until bubbles cover the surface of the pancakes, and their undersides are lightly browned. Gently turn
them over and cook for 1 to 2 minutes more, until the other
sides are browned. Serve with warm maple syrup, sour cream,
or jam.

# Phil's Famous Potato Latkes

*About 12 latkes; serves 2 to 4*

Potato latkes are best known as a Chanukah specialty. Like most Jewish holiday foods, latkes have symbolic value: because they are fried in oil, they are a reminder of the first Chanukah oil lamp, the menorah, which is said to have burned miraculously for eight days using only a day's worth of oil.

This recipe comes from Steve's father, Philip Siegelman, for whom latkes are somewhere between a science and a religious calling. After years of experimentation, he hit upon the rather unorthodox idea of adding a small amount of grated cheese to the batter, an innovation that doesn't much affect the flavor of the pancakes, but gives them a surprisingly crispy texture and beautiful golden brown color. (Purists may omit the cheese—the results are still outstanding.)

Because potatoes vary in size and water content, you'll need to adjust the amount of flour you use. Use high-quality, fresh oil and always make sure it is hot enough before adding the batter. This will make the difference between light, crispy latkes and soggy, greasy ones.

*1 pound russet potatoes (about 2 large), peeled*
*1/2 large yellow onion*
*1 egg, lightly beaten*
*1/4 to 1/2 cup all-purpose flour*
*1 teaspoon baking powder*
*1/2 teaspoon salt*
*2 tablespoons shredded Swiss or Monterey Jack cheese*
  *(optional)*
*Vegetable oil, for frying*
*Applesauce and sour cream, for serving*

Grate the potatoes and onion into a large bowl, using the medium-fine holes of a hand grater to produce a pulpy mush. Add the egg, 1/4 cup of the flour, the baking powder, salt, and cheese, stirring to just to combine. The batter should be fairly liquid, about the consistency of chunky applesauce. If it looks too thin, add up to 1/4 cup more flour.

Pour the oil into a heavy skillet or sauté pan to a depth of about 1/4 inch and heat over medium-high heat. Test the temperature by dropping a teaspoonful of the batter into the oil; it should sizzle immediately and begin to brown after 30 seconds. When the oil is hot, spoon the batter by scant 1/4-cup measures into the skillet, spacing them apart and pressing the pancakes down gently to make them flat and round. Fry for 3 to 5 minutes, until the edges look crisp and the undersides are nicely browned. Carefully turn them over and cook for 2 to 3 minutes more, until browned. Transfer to paper towels to drain. Repeat with the remaining batter, adding oil to the skillet as needed to maintain a 1/4-inch depth.

Serve immediately, or place the cooked pancakes on a baking sheet between layers of paper towels and keep warm in a 250°F oven for up to 15 minutes. Serve with applesauce and sour cream.

# Manfred's Mom's Kartoffelpuffer

*About 12 (4-inch) pancakes; serves 4*

Potatoes are a cornerstone of the American diner menu, and Bette's is a case in point. Our customers can't seem to get enough of them. Every week, we turn a monumental one thousand pounds of potatoes into home fries, potato salad, corned beef hash, and, of course, potato pancakes.

Bette's husband, Manfred, grew up on a small family farm outside Hamburg, Germany. For Sunday dinner, his mother, Ursula, would prepare red cabbage and pork chops, served with *Kartoffelpuffer*—golden brown, crispy potato pancakes. Her simple recipe has been a signature dish at the Diner from the day we opened. We grate our potatoes to order for these pancakes so they're always fresh tasting and crisp. We serve them for breakfast with homemade applesauce and sour cream, or as a lunch special with grilled bockwurst and applesauce.

> *2 eggs, beaten*
> *1/4 cup all-purpose flour*
> *1/4 cup grated yellow onion*
> *1 teaspoon salt*
> *1/2 teaspoon freshly ground black pepper*
> *2 pounds russet potatoes (about 4 large), peeled*
> *1/4 cup vegetable oil, for frying*
> *Applesauce and sour cream, for serving*

In a bowl, combine the eggs, flour, onion, salt, and pepper and stir to blend. Shred the potatoes into a separate bowl, using the largest holes of a hand grater. Using your hands, squeeze out as much liquid as you can from the potatoes. Add the potatoes to the egg mixture and mix well.

In a large, heavy skillet, heat 1 to 2 tablespoons of the oil over medium-high heat. When the oil is hot, spoon the batter by 1/4-cup measures into the skillet, spacing them apart and pressing the pancakes down gently to make them flat and round. Fry for 3 to 5 minutes, until the undersides of the pancakes are nicely browned. Gently turn them over and cook for about 3 minutes longer, until the other sides are browned. Transfer to paper towels to drain. Repeat with the remaining batter, adding oil to the skillet as needed. Serve immediately with applesauce and sour cream.

# Crêpes

Crêpes are an international snack. Parisians make a quick meal of them at tiny food stands, where the fillings range from ham and Gruyère cheese to jam, Grand Marnier, or the elegantly simple crêpe *nature* rolled in butter and vanilla sugar. In Brittany, crisp, hearty buckwheat galettes are filled with seafood and other savory and sweet fillings. The Russians fill their *blinchiki* with a cottage cheese or fruit stuffing. In Italy, delicate *crespelle* are rolled around savory meat or cheese fillings. And in Hungary, *palacsintas* are an everyday food served even in the humblest of households.

Somehow, Americans have come to view crêpes as a fancy delicacy. Don't be intimidated. Crêpes are a delicious treat, and they're not hard to master. They're really nothing more than unleavened, paper-thin pancakes made of flour, milk, eggs, and butter. The batter is poured sparingly into a pan and cooked quickly.

Unlike classic pancake batter, crêpe batter needs to be beaten so that the gluten in the flour develops (a blender works well for this), which gives crêpes their delicate strength. It should then be chilled for an hour or more to allow the gluten to relax. The best crêpes are strong enough to hold a loose filling while still remaining soft and tender to the bite. They are served rolled, folded, or stacked.

The ideal tool for making crêpes is a French-style crêpe pan—a flat iron or steel pan with low, sloping sides, measuring about six inches across the bottom and lightweight enough to be turned easily as you pour in the batter. It's not essential though; you can also use a heavy nonstick pan with sloping sides. At the Diner, we've been using the same set of inexpensive French steel omelet pans for more than twenty years. They stay seasoned, never stick, and are light and easy to hold.

Crêpe batter should be about the consistency of buttermilk, just thick enough to coat the ladle. Your first crêpe is likely to be a throwaway tester that will tell you whether your batter is thin enough to swirl properly (if it's not, add a little cold water) and whether the pan is hot enough. When the temperature of the pan is just right, the batter will adhere to it in a thin, uniform layer.

As with most pancakes, the first side of the crêpe to be cooked is more evenly browned and attractive than the second, so you'll generally want to roll or fold crêpes with the first side facing out.

Crêpes can be made ahead of time, stacked, wrapped in plastic wrap, and stored for up to forty-eight hours at room temperature or in the refrigerator. They can also be stacked between layers of waxed paper, wrapped in foil, and frozen for up to two months.

# Classic Crêpes

*About 16 (7-inch) crêpes; serves 4 to 8*

This basic crêpe batter works well for both sweet and savory fillings (see the following pages). Made in a blender, it's quick to prepare in advance.

At Bette's, we mainly use these crêpes to make blintzes (page 80), cooking them on one side only, then rolling them around a cottage cheese filling with the uncooked side facing out. With six pans fired up at once, one cook can turn out fifty or more blintz wrappers in just twenty minutes. It's quite a sight. We make these at night for the following morning, turning them out onto cotton towels, then stacking them as they cool.

> $^3/_4$ cup cold water
> $^1/_2$ cup cold milk
> 2 eggs
> $^1/_4$ cup butter, melted
> $^1/_2$ teaspoon salt
> 1 cup all-purpose flour

Combine the water, milk, eggs, butter, salt, and flour, in that order, in a blender. Blend at top speed for 30 seconds. Scrape down any lumps from the sides of the blender container with a rubber spatula. Blend for 15 seconds more, until smooth. (If you don't have a blender, combine the ingredients in a bowl and beat with a wire whisk or electric mixer until well blended.) Cover and chill the batter for at least 1 hour or overnight.

Heat a crêpe pan over medium heat and wipe it with vegetable oil. Ladle in about 3 tablespoons of the batter, enough to barely cover the pan, swirling the pan to evenly coat the bottom and partway up the sides. Cook for 1 to 2 minutes, until the edges begin to pull away from the pan and the bottom of the crêpe is lightly browned. Turn the crêpe over and continue cooking for about 30 seconds, until the other side is lightly browned. Remove the crêpe from the pan and repeat, oiling the pan as needed and stacking the cooked crêpes.

# Sweet Crêpes

## CRÊPES NATURE

This is the simplest and most delicate of crêpe desserts. Brush the second side of a crêpe with 1/2 teaspoon softened butter and sprinkle it with 1/2 teaspoon vanilla sugar (see box). Fold the crêpe into quarters with the first side facing out. Sprinkle with a little additional vanilla sugar. Serve on warm plates, allowing 2 crêpes per serving.

## LEMON CRÊPES LUCIE

Bette and Manfred's daughter, Lucie, has enjoyed these simple crêpes all over France. Sprinkle the second side of a crêpe with freshly squeezed lemon juice and 1/2 teaspoon sugar. Fold the crêpe into quarters with the first side facing out. Sprinkle with a little additional sugar. Serve on warm plates, allowing 2 crêpes per serving.

## COCONUT "FANCAKES"

When Steve was a kid, his family spent a year in India. Their cook, Muragesan, was wonderfully inventive, working southern Indian ingredients into the French cuisine he had picked up while cooking for diplomats. Among his finest East-West creations were delicate coconut crêpes, which he called coconut "fancakes," named not for their fanlike shape but because Muragesan could not pronounce the letter "p." (He also made a delicious "phoenix" pudding from ground peanuts.)

Sprinkle the second side of a crêpe with freshly squeezed lime juice and toasted, sweetened shredded coconut. Fold the crêpe into quarters and dust with confectioners' sugar. Serve on warm plates, allowing 2 crêpes per serving.

---

### Vanilla Sugar

Split a vanilla bean lengthwise and place it in an airtight container with a cup of sugar. Remove the vanilla bean after one week and reserve it for another use. The sugar will be deliciously perfumed and flavorful. In a pinch, you can also make vanilla sugar by thoroughly combining 1 cup sugar with 1/2 teaspoon pure vanilla extract.

## SUNDAE CRÊPES

Fold two crêpes into quarters and place them, slightly overlapping, on a plate; top with a scoop of vanilla ice cream and a generous drizzle of hot fudge sauce. Sprinkle with toasted sliced almonds.

## JAM CRÊPES

Spread crêpes with jam, roll up, and eat. Kids love these. Along these same lines, Nutella, peanut butter and honey, or chestnut butter also make delicious fillings for warm crêpes.

# Savory Crêpes

You can fill crêpes with just about anything. They take particularly well to creamy fillings, like creamed mushrooms, spinach, seafood, or chicken. They're also delicious filled with diced ham and Gruyère cheese, asparagus, ratatouille, goat cheese, or herbed cream cheese. Anything that makes a good filling for an omelet will work well when rolled into a crêpe.

You can prepare most filled or rolled crêpes several hours ahead of time, arranging them in a single layer in a buttered baking dish. Dot them with a little butter or spoon some béchamel sauce over them. Reheat the crêpes in a 350°F oven for 10 to 15 minutes, until they have begun to brown lightly and are warmed through.

# Breton Buckwheat Galettes

*About 20 (7-inch) crêpes; serves 4 to 8*

The buckwheat crêpes of Brittany are heartier and a little crisper than the classic Parisian version. Ours are made with beer and buttermilk, which complement the tanginess of the buckwheat perfectly. Both sweet and savory fillings go well with these crêpes.

> *3 eggs*
> *1 cup buttermilk*
> *1 cup medium-bodied beer*
> *1/4 cup water*
> *1/4 cup butter, melted*
> *1 cup all-purpose flour*
> *1/3 cup buckwheat flour*
> *2 teaspoons sugar*
> *1/4 teaspoon salt*

Combine the eggs, buttermilk, beer, water, butter, all-purpose flour, buckwheat flour, sugar, and salt, in that order, in a blender. Blend at top speed for about 30 seconds. Scrape down any lumps from the sides of the blender container with a rubber spatula. Blend for 30 seconds more, or until the batter is well mixed. (If you don't have a blender, combine all the ingredients in a bowl and beat with a wire whisk or electric mixer until well blended.) Cover and chill the batter for at least 1 hour or overnight.

Heat a crêpe pan over medium heat and wipe it with vegetable oil. Ladle in about 3 tablespoons of the batter, enough to barely cover the pan, tilting and swirling the pan to evenly coat the bottom and partway up the sides. Cook for 1 to 2 minutes, until the edges begin to pull away from the pan and the bottom of the galette is lightly browned. Turn over and continue cooking for about 30 seconds, until the other side is lightly browned. Remove the galette from the pan and repeat the process, oiling the pan as needed and stacking the cooked galettes.

# Ham and Cheese Crêpe Gâteau

*Serves 4 to 6*

This makes an elegant first course or a nice brunch entrée. For a lighter presentation, serve with crème fraîche or a little Dijon mustard in place of the cream sauce.

> 1 cup shredded Gruyère cheese
> 1/2 cup grated Parmesan cheese
> 16 Classic Crêpes (page 74)
> 1/4 cup butter, melted
> 1 to 2 tablespoons Dijon mustard
> 15 very thin slices Westphalian or Black Forest ham (about 12 ounces)
> 2 cups heavy cream

Preheat the oven to 375°F. Line a baking sheet with aluminum foil.

In a small bowl, combine the cheeses and set aside. Place one crêpe with the first side facing up on the prepared baking sheet. Brush the crêpe with a small amount of butter. Spread about 1/4 teaspoon mustard over the crêpe and sprinkle on 1 heaping tablespoon of the cheese mixture. Place a slice of ham over the cheese, pulling it apart slightly if necessary to cover the crêpe to the edges. Place another crêpe on top of the ham and continue layering with butter, mustard, cheese, and ham until all the crêpes are used, ending with a crêpe. Brush the top of the stack with butter. Bake for about 20 minutes, until the top is nicely browned.

To make the sauce, bring the cream to a rolling boil in a heavy saucepan over medium-high heat. Decrease the heat to achieve a gentle boil and continue to cook for 10 to 15 minutes, until reduced by half.

Cut the hot gâteau into wedges. Pool 2 or 3 tablespoons of the warm sauce on each plate and place a slice of the gâteau over the sauce. Serve immediately.

# Spinach Crespelle

*16 crespelle; serves 4 to 6*

*Crespelle* are the Italian answer to crêpes, and they're some-times rolled, blintz-style, around a sweet or savory filling. Our spinach *crespelle* are a popular lunch special at the Diner. They can be served with a light dusting of Parmesan cheese or a little warm tomato sauce.

> *1 pound ricotta cheese*
> *1 cup chopped cooked spinach (about 1 pound raw),*
>   *squeezed dry*
> *1/4 cup grated Parmesan cheese*
> *2 tablespoons finely chopped green onions*
> *3 tablespoons chopped toasted pecans*
> *1 egg yolk, beaten*
> *Pinch of nutmeg*
> *Salt and freshly cracked black pepper*
> *16 Classic Crêpes, cooked on one side only (page 74)*
> *2 to 3 tablespoons butter*

To make the filling, in a bowl, combine the ricotta, spinach, Parmesan, green onions, pecans, egg yolk, and nutmeg and mix well. Season with salt and pepper.

To assemble the *crespelle,* place a crêpe, cooked side up, on a clean surface. Spoon 2 tablespoons of the filling onto the edge of the crêpe nearest you. Fold the sides over the filling, then roll the *crespelle* away from you, ending with the seam side facing down. Repeat with the remaining crêpes and filling.

Heat 1 tablespoon of the butter in a large nonstick sauté pan over medium-high heat. Place a few *crespelle* in the pan, seam sides down and about 1/2 inch apart. Avoid crowding too many into the pan. Fry, turning once, for 3 to 4 minutes on each side, until the *crespelle* are nicely browned. Repeat until all the *crespelle* are browned, adding more butter to the pan as needed.

# Cheese Blintzes

*16 blintzes; serves 4*

Blintzes aren't really pancakes, but because they're made from crêpes—and we love them—we're including them. If you've mastered crêpe making, you're ready to try blintzes, which are nothing more than crêpes that have been cooked on one side only, then wrapped around a simple sweet or savory filling, with the cooked side facing in. You can prepare the crêpes well in advance (up to a day), fill and roll the blintzes a few hours before you plan to serve them, and then brown them at the last minute.

Farmer cheese or pot cheese (drier versions of cottage cheese) are ideal for a blintz filling. Conventional large-curd cottage cheese can also be used, but it should be drained for an hour or more in the refrigerator in a fine-mesh strainer set over a bowl. This helps the filling hold together better, and produces blintzes with a delicately firm texture. If you don't have time to drain cottage cheese, you can replace a third of it with ricotta. At the Diner, we serve blintzes with sour cream and fruit preserves (berry or cherry are best). They're also wonderful with warm Blueberry Compote Topping (page 103).

> *3 cups farmer cheese or pot cheese; or 3 cups large-curd*
> *cottage cheese, drained for 1 hour or more in a fine-mesh*
> *strainer; or 2 cups large-curd cottage cheese and 1 cup*
> *ricotta cheese*
> *2 egg yolks*
> *1 1/2 tablespoons sugar*
> *1 1/2 teaspoons freshly grated lemon zest*
> *1 teaspoon pure vanilla extract*
> *16 Classic Crêpes, cooked on one side only (page 74)*
> *2 to 3 tablespoons butter*
> *Sour cream and fruit preserves, for serving*

To make the filling, in a bowl, combine the cheese, egg yolks, sugar, lemon zest, and vanilla and mix well.

To assemble the blintzes, place a crêpe, cooked side up, on a clean surface. Spoon 2 tablespoons of the filling onto the end of the crêpe nearest you. Fold the sides over the filling, then roll the blintz away from you, ending with the seam side facing down. Repeat with the remaining crêpes and filling.

Heat 1 tablespoon of the butter in a large nonstick sauté pan over medium-high heat. Place a few blintzes in the pan, seam sides down and about 1/2 inch apart. Avoid crowding too many into the pan. Fry, turning once, for 3 to 4 minutes on each side, until the blintzes are nicely browned. Repeat until all the blintzes are browned, adding more butter to the pan as needed. Serve with sour cream and preserves.

# Suzette's Crêpes Suzette

Crêpes Suzette is the showgirl of the pancake family. Drenched in a luxurious orange butter sauce and flambéed dramatically at the table, Crêpes Suzette was once the elegant dessert par excellence at dinner parties and fancy "Continental" restaurants. We think it's time it staged a comeback. It not only tastes unbelievably good, it's so dramatic and amusing that the performance never fails to make people smile. Don't forget to dim the lights for the full effect.

This recipe comes from our own Suzette, Diner cofounder Sue Conley.

*16 Classic Crêpes (page 74)*
*1 cup freshly squeezed orange juice*
*1 tablespoon grated orange zest*
*1/2 cup butter*
*1/3 cup plus 1 teaspoon sugar*
*1/3 cup orange liqueur, such as Grand Marnier*

Preheat the oven to 400°F. Butter a large ovenproof serving dish with sides at least 1 1/2 inches high.

Fold the crêpes into quarters with the first sides facing out and arrange them, overlapping slightly, in the prepared serving dish.

To make the sauce, combine the orange juice, zest, butter, and the 1/3 cup sugar in a heavy saucepan. Place over medium-high heat and bring the mixture to a boil. Decrease the heat to achieve a simmer and cook, stirring occasionally, for 5 to 10 minutes, until the sauce is syrupy and has reduced to about 1 1/4 cups. (The recipe can be made several hours ahead up to this point; reheat the sauce before using.)

Pour the hot sauce over the crêpes in the dish, sprinkle the 1 teaspoon sugar over the top, and place the dish in the oven. Bake for 5 to 10 minutes, until the crêpes are warmed through and the sauce is bubbling.

Place the liqueur in a small, deep saucepan over medium heat until warmed through.

Bring the crêpes and the warmed liqueur to the table on a metal or foil-lined tray to catch any spills. Pour the liqueur over the crêpes, light a long match, stand back, and carefully ignite the surface of the sauce. Serve as soon as the flames— and the applause—have subsided.

# Swedish Pancakes Erickson

*12 to 14 (6-inch) pancakes; serves 3 to 4*

You've heard of Chicken Tetrazzini? Peach Melba? These famous dishes were named for great operatic divas. We like this tradition, and we've named our Swedish pancakes in memory of our own Diner diva, soprano Kaaren Erickson Sooter, a longtime friend and customer whose career included such high points as an impromptu concert at the Diner and singing lead roles at the Metropolitan Opera. This is her Uncle Oskar's traditional recipe. Kaaren remembered how her mother would turn these pancakes out in rapid succession while the hungry kids snatched them up and ate them with their fingers.

Swedish pancakes are also known as *plättar*. They are delicate, eggy, and extremely thin, more like a crêpe than a pancake. Although Swedish pancakes are traditionally made in a *plättpan*—a special cast-iron skillet with three-inch round depressions into which the batter is poured to make tiny, perfectly round cakes—a small nonstick sauté pan also works well.

*4 eggs*
*1 cup milk*
*1/2 teaspoon sugar*
*1/4 teaspoon salt*
*1/4 cup all-purpose flour*
*Melted butter, for greasing the pan*

## FOR SERVING

*Confectioners' sugar*
*Canned lingonberries or lingonberry preserves*

Place the eggs, milk, sugar, salt, and flour, in that order, in a blender. Blend at top speed for about 30 seconds. Scrape down any lumps from the sides of the blender container with a rubber spatula. Blend for 15 seconds more, until smooth. (If you don't have a blender, combine all the ingredients in a bowl and beat with a wire whisk or electric mixer until they are well blended.) Cover and refrigerate the batter for at least 1 hour or overnight.

Heat a 6-inch nonstick sauté pan over medium heat and wipe it with melted butter. Ladle in about 3 tablespoons of the batter, enough to barely cover the pan, tilting and swirling the pan to evenly coat the bottom and partway up the sides. Cook for 1 to 2 minutes, until the underside is lightly browned. Turn over and cook for 30 seconds, until the other side is lightly browned. Slide the pancake from the pan and flip it so that the first side is facing down. Immediately sprinkle the pancake with confectioners' sugar, spread about a tablespoonful of lingonberries over the surface, and roll the pancake up tightly. Dust with a little more confectioners' sugar and eat right away. Repeat with the remaining batter, wiping the pan with a little butter before cooking each pancake.

# Pancakes
## FROM THE Oven

P ancakes made in the oven or broiler are dramatic and impressive—a great choice for entertaining. They're also surprisingly easy to throw together, and don't require you to stand guard over a hot griddle, because most or all of the cooking takes place in the oven or under the broiler.

In this chapter, we've included our two favorite types of oven pancakes: the soufflé pancake made with beaten egg whites, and the simple yet spectacular Dutch Bunny.

Traditionally, soufflés are made with a béchamel (white sauce) enriched with egg yolks and lightened with beaten egg whites. To fit the rapid pace of short-order cooking, we developed the soufflé pancake, a speedy "pan soufflé," which starts on the stovetop and is finished under the broiler. In the early years of the Diner, we served two flavors, banana-rum and apple-brandy; over time, we've added a range of savory and dessert versions, all based on the same versatile batter and cooking method. You'll find some of our favorites following the base soufflé pancake recipe.

# Bette's Diner Soufflé Pancakes

*1 (8-inch) pancake; serves 1 or 2*

This is the show-stopper of our breakfast menu. We've been serving these soufflé pancakes since we opened the Diner, and they've become a signature dish that people tell their friends about and order week after week.

When these pancakes are removed from the broiler, they are beautifully puffed and browned. You'll need to watch carefully during the last few minutes of cooking to make sure that the soufflé doesn't get overcooked. An overcooked soufflé will fall immediately; one that is perfectly cooked will stay high and puffy all the way to the table. As the pancake cools, the center will continue to cook. Instruct your guests on the proper way to eat a soufflé pancake: edges first, center last.

*2 egg yolks*
*1/2 cup half-and-half*
*1/4 cup all-purpose flour*
*1 1/2 tablespoons butter, melted*
*1/2 teaspoon sugar*
*1/4 teaspoon salt*
*3 egg whites*

Preheat the broiler.

In a large bowl, beat the egg yolks with the half-and-half. Add the flour slowly, stirring just to combine. Stir in the butter, sugar, and salt. (At this point, add to the batter those ingredients specified in your chosen recipe; see variations following.) Place the egg whites in a separate bowl. With an electric mixer or whisk, beat until the whites form soft peaks. Gently fold the whites into the batter, just until combined.

Heat a lightly buttered 10-inch nonstick sauté pan with an ovenproof handle, or a heavy cast-iron skillet, over high heat until it is almost smoking. Pour the batter into the pan. Decrease the heat to medium and cook for about 5 minutes,

*(continued)*

until the bottom of the pancake is nicely browned and the batter has begun to firm up.

Arrange the pieces of prepared fruit, nuts, or other ingredients called for in your chosen recipe in a circular pattern on top of the batter, laying them gently on the surface. Place the pan 4 to 5 inches below the broiler element and cook for 2 to 4 minutes, watching carefully to avoid burning, until the pancake is puffed, the top is browned, and the center is just set but still soft.

Gently slide the pancake onto a warmed serving plate, dust the fruit and dessert variations with confectioners' sugar, and whisk to the table. Serve immediately with butter and warm maple syrup or other toppings, as indicated in your chosen recipe.

# Fruit Soufflé Pancakes

### APPLE-BRANDY

Heat 1 tablespoon butter in a small sauté pan over medium heat. Add 1 cup peeled, cored, sliced apple (1 large apple) and 1/4 teaspoon ground cinnamon. Sauté for 2 to 4 minutes, until just soft.

To the batter, add 1 tablespoon applejack, Calvados, or other brandy. Top the half-cooked pancake with the sautéed apples just before placing it under the broiler.

### BANANA-RUM

To the batter, add 1 tablespoon dark rum. Top the half-cooked pancake with 1 cup banana slices (1 large banana) just before placing it under the broiler.

## PEAR WILLIAM

Heat 1 tablespoon butter in a small sauté pan over medium heat. Add 1 cup peeled, cored, sliced pear (1 large pear; firm pears, such as Bosc or Anjou, work well) and a few drops of pure vanilla extract. Sauté for 2 to 4 minutes, until just soft.

To the batter, add 1 tablespoon pear brandy. Top the half-cooked pancake with the sautéed pears just before placing it under the broiler.

## FRESH BERRY AND GRAND MARNIER

To the batter, add 1 tablespoon Grand Marnier liqueur. In a bowl, toss 1 cup fresh blueberries, blackberries, raspberries, or sliced strawberries, or a combination of any of these, with 1 tablespoon sugar. Stir the berries into the batter; reserving a few to place on top of the half-cooked pancake before it goes under the broiler.

## PINEAPPLE-MANGO

Peel and core a pineapple and quarter lengthwise. Cut each quarter crosswise into 1/4-inch-thick slices. Peel and pit a mango and cut into 1/4-inch-thick slices.

To the batter, add 1 tablespoon dark rum. Top the half-cooked pancake with 6 to 8 pineapple slices and 6 to 8 mango slices just before placing it under the broiler.

## PEACH MELBA

Press 1/2 cup fresh or thawed frozen raspberries through a strainer to make a sauce. Add sugar to taste. Peel and pit a large, ripe, firm peach and cut into 1/4-inch slices.

To the batter, add 1 tablespoon peach schnapps. Top the half-cooked pancake with the peach slices just before placing it under the broiler. Serve with the raspberry sauce and whipped cream.

# Dessert Soufflé Pancakes

## CHOCOLATE

To the batter, add 2 tablespoons chocolate syrup, 1/4 cup chocolate chips, and 2 tablespoons dark rum (optional). Sprinkle the half-cooked pancake with a few additional chocolate chips just before placing it under the broiler. Dust with confectioners' sugar before serving.

## NUTTY PRALINE

To the batter, add 2 tablespoons dark rum. Bring 2 tablespoons sugar, 2 tablespoons water, and a few drops of freshly squeezed lemon juice to a boil over medium-high heat in the pan you will be using for the pancake. Continue to boil for about 4 minutes, until the sugar is lightly caramelized. Stir in 1/4 cup chopped pecans. Cook 1 minute more and remove the pan from the heat. Remove the caramelized pecans and reserve a few for garnish. Return the pan to the stove top over high heat and add 2 teaspoons butter. Heat until almost smoking. Distribute the caramelized pecans in the pan and immediately pour the batter over the pecans. Sprinkle the reserved pecans over the half-cooked pancake just before placing it under the broiler. Dust with confectioners' sugar and serve with maple syrup or warm caramel sauce.

> ### Caramelizing Sugar
>
> When caramelizing sugar, add a few drops of lemon juice to keep the sugar from crystallizing.

# Savory Soufflé Pancakes

To make wonderful savory soufflé pancakes that are perfect for brunch or a light dinner, substitute 1/2 teaspoon dry mustard for the sugar in the soufflé pancake recipe on page 89. If desired, add a pinch of cayenne pepper to the batter. These savory variations cook faster than the sweet versions and only need about 3 minutes under the broiler. Watch carefully to avoid overcooking.

## CHILE-CHEESE

To the batter, add 1/2 cup grated Cheddar, Monterey Jack, or Swiss cheese and 1/2 cup diced, peeled, roasted fresh pasilla or Anaheim chiles, or red bell peppers. Reserve a few of the diced chiles to sprinkle over the half-cooked pancake just before placing it under the broiler.

## CRAB AND AVOCADO

To the batter, add 1/2 cup cooked crabmeat and 1/2 ripe avocado cut into 1/2-inch chunks.

## GREEN ONION AND BACON

Cook, drain, and crumble 3 strips of bacon. To the batter, add the crumbled bacon and 1/4 cup thinly sliced green onions.

## HAM AND CHEESE

To the batter, add 1/2 cup grated Gruyère or Cheddar cheese. Sprinkle the half-cooked pancake with 1/4 cup diced ham just before it goes under the broiler.

# Dutch Bunny

*Serves 2 to 4*

The Dutch Bunny is a minor miracle. It's really nothing more than eggs, milk, butter, and flour baked in a hot oven. But if you've never made one, you're in for a surprise. The thin, liquid batter—much like popover or Yorkshire pudding batter—cooks quickly, producing lots of steam, and the result is an enormously puffed pancake with crusty brown edges; a soft, eggy center; and a rich and buttery flavor.

There's really nothing Dutch (or, for that matter, bunny-like) about Dutch Bunnies. In fact, they were brought to America by early German settlers. Their name is probably a corruption of *deutsche* and possibly *Pfanne*, the German word for pan. The traditional German version is made with apples, and we've provided that variation as well.

A Dutch Bunny makes a nice finish to a light brunch. It's also fun to serve as a late evening snack (we recommend it with champagne on New Year's Eve) and it's just the thing to whip up for unexpected guests. Few recipes this simple deliver such stunning results from such basic ingredients.

*3 eggs*
*3/4 cup milk*
*3/4 cup all-purpose flour*
*1/2 teaspoon salt*
*6 tablespoons butter*

## FOR SERVING

*Juice of 1/2 lemon*
*Confectioners' sugar*
*Apricot preserves or maple syrup*

Preheat the oven to 450°F. In a bowl, beat the eggs and milk until well blended. Add the flour and salt all at once, stirring just to combine. The batter will be slightly lumpy.

Melt the butter in a heavy 12-inch sauté pan with an ovenproof handle or in a 9 by 13-inch oval baking dish. When the butter is very hot and just beginning to brown, pour the batter into the pan and immediately transfer to the oven. Bake for 20 minutes, or until the pancake is golden brown and puffed.

Assemble the guests and bring the pancake to the table immediately (the pancake will begin to deflate quickly). Sprinkle the pancake with lemon juice and confectioners' sugar. Cut into wedges and serve with preserves or syrup.

## GERMAN APPLE PANCAKE

Peel, core, and slice 2 tart apples. In a bowl, toss the apples with 3 tablespoons sugar, 2 tablespoons freshly squeezed lemon juice, and 1/4 teaspoon ground cinnamon. Melt 2 table-spoons butter in a heavy skillet or sauté pan over medium heat. Add the apples and sauté for 2 to 4 minutes, until just soft. Heat 4 tablespoons butter in a heavy sauté pan or oval baking dish as directed in the Dutch Bunny recipe. Spread the apples in the bottom of the pan or dish. Pour the batter over the sautéed apples and transfer the pan to the oven. Bake for 20 minutes, or until the pancake is golden brown and puffed. Sprinkle with lemon juice and dust with confectioners' sugar.

## DUTCH BABIES

Divide either of the recipes above among 4 (6-inch) skillets. Bake for about 15 minutes.

# Kids' Pancakes

Pancakes have always been particularly popular with our younger customers. Here are a few simple ideas to try on yours. Use our basic buttermilk pancake recipe (page 24), which yields about 24 (4-inch) pancakes, or any of our pancake mixes.

## Mickey Mouse Pancakes

Pour enough batter onto the griddle to make a normal-sized pancake; immediately ladle 2 more tiny circles of batter so that they attach themselves to the first pancake to make mouse ears. Before serving, place raisins on each pancake to make the eyes and nose, and add a strawberry slice for the mouth.

## Snowman Pancakes

Using the same technique described for Mickey Mouse Pancakes, make 3 circles, one above the other, each slightly smaller than the one before. Use raisins or currants to make a face and buttons.

## Alphabet Pancakes

Make pancakes shaped like letters to spell out names or initials. Remember that the letters need to be poured onto the griddle in mirror writing, so that they will read right when the pancakes are flipped.

## Cartoon Pancakes

Thin some pancake batter with a little milk and put it in a squeeze bottle. Use this batter to draw a small, simple cartoon on the griddle. Choose something with a clear outline—a face, a picture of an animal, and so on. Allow to cook for 30 to 45 seconds before ladling regular pancake batter over it, so that the batter fills in the drawing right up to the outline. When you flip the pancake, your line drawing will appear darker on its surface.

# Pineapple Upside-Down Cakes

Place a pineapple ring on the griddle. Put a cherry in the center of the ring. Ladle 1/4 cup pancake batter over the pineapple and cook as directed for buttermilk pancakes.

# Granola Griddle Cakes

Sprinkle a little granola into pancake batter for added crunch and sweetness.

# Silver Dollar Pancakes

Kids can't resist miniature food. Use 1 to 2 tablespoons of batter per pancake.

# Pancake Sandwiches

Spread jam, jelly, or a combination of peanut butter and jelly on a cooked pancake. Top with a second pancake. Allow the sandwiches to cool slightly so that kids can eat them with their hands.

# Chocolate Chip Pancakes

Add mini chocolate chips and chopped toasted walnuts to the pancake batter before cooking.

## Freezing Pancakes

Pancakes and waffles can be frozen and reheated with perfectly acceptable results, so you can whip them up for hungry kids in a few minutes. To freeze, allow cooked pancakes or waffles to cool completely, then wrap them individually in plastic wrap or plastic bags.

Reheat them in a toaster oven, conventional oven, or microwave.

# Simple Pancake Toppings

New customers at Bette's Diner are often delighted by the unexpected extra touches we add to our plates, like a hot or cold topping with their pancakes or waffles. The same principle works well at home. Taking a few minutes to whip up a simple topping turns your favorite pancake into the special of the day.

# WARM TOPPINGS

Serve these toppings immediately, or refrigerate and reheat them before serving.

## Citrus-Maple Syrup

*Serves 4 to 6*

1/2 cup pure maple syrup
1/2 teaspoon freshly grated orange or lemon zest
2 tablespoons butter

In a heavy saucepan, combine the syrup and zest over medium-high heat. Bring to a boil, then decrease the heat and simmer for 1 minute. Stir in the butter until melted.

# Blueberry Compote Topping

*Serves 4 to 6*

*2 cups fresh or frozen blueberries*
*1/2 cup freshly squeezed orange juice*
*1 teaspoon cornstarch dissolved in 1/4 cup water*
*1/2 teaspoon freshly grated orange zest*
*2 tablespoons sugar*

In a heavy saucepan, combine the blueberries, orange juice, cornstarch solution, zest, and sugar over medium-high heat. Heat, stirring occasionally, for 4 to 5 minutes, until the syrup comes to a boil. Remove the pan from the heat; the sauce will thicken as it cools. Serve warm.

# Emergency "Maple Syrup"

*Serves 4 to 6*

*1 1/2 cups firmly packed brown sugar*
*1/2 cup water*
*1/4 cup butter*
*1/2 teaspoon pure vanilla extract*

In a heavy saucepan, combine the sugar and water over medium-high heat. Heat, stirring, for about 5 minutes, until the syrup comes to a boil. Remove the pan from the heat and stir in the butter and vanilla until the butter melts.

# Warm Apple-Currant Topping

*Serves 4 to 6*

*2 large tart apples, such as Granny Smith, peeled, cored, and
cut into 1/4-inch dice (about 2 cups)*
*1/4 cup currants*
*2 tablespoons maple syrup or brown sugar*
*1/4 cup water*
*1 tablespoon butter*
*1 tablespoon freshly squeezed lemon juice*
*1/2 teaspoon ground cinnamon*

In a heavy saucepan, combine all the ingredients over low
heat. Cover the pan and simmer, stirring occasionally, for
about 10 minutes, until the apples are soft but still hold their
shape.

# Apple Cider Syrup

*Serves 4 to 6*

*8 cups apple cider or apple juice*
*1/4 teaspoon ground cinnamon*

In a large, heavy-bottomed pot, combine the cider and cinnamon and bring to a boil over high heat. Boil for 10 to 15 minutes, until the liquid is reduced by half. Skim off any foam,
decrease the heat to medium, and boil gently for 1 to 2 hours,
until reduced to about 1 cup of liquid with the consistency of
maple syrup. The syrup will solidify as it cools, but will
become pourable again when reheated. Serve warm. (Packed
in jars, this syrup makes a nice gift and will keep for a month
or more in the refrigerator.)

# Warm Orange Sauce

*Serves 4 to 6*

*1 cup freshly squeezed orange juice*
*1 tablespoon grated orange zest*
*1/2 cup butter*
*1/3 cup sugar*

In a heavy saucepan, combine the orange juice, zest, butter, and sugar over medium-high heat. Bring to a boil, decrease the heat to low, and simmer, stirring occasionally, for 5 to 10 minutes, until the sauce is syrupy.

## Warm Honey Syrup

Honey, heated to the boiling point, will become thin and pourable, making a delicious syrup for pancakes and waffles. If desired, add a small amount of ground cinnamon while heating.

# COLD TOPPINGS

All of these toppings can be made several hours ahead of time and refrigerated. The butters should be brought to room temperature before serving.

## Cranberries and Cream

*Serves 4 to 6*

*1 (16-ounce) can whole-berry cranberry sauce, or 2 cups homemade cranberry sauce*
*1 cup sour cream or plain yogurt*

In a bowl, combine the cranberry sauce and sour cream or yogurt and mix well. Cover and refrigerate until chilled.

## Whipped Honey Butter

*Serves 4 to 6*

*1 cup unsalted butter, at room temperature*
*1 cup honey*

Place the butter in a bowl. Using an electric mixer on medium-high speed, beat the butter until soft and fluffy. Beat in the honey and continue to beat until thoroughly combined.

# Lemon–Poppy Seed Butter

### Serves 4 to 6

*1 cup unsalted butter, at room temperature*
*1/2 cup confectioners' sugar*
*2 teaspoons poppy seeds*
*1 teaspoon freshly grated lemon zest*

Place the butter and sugar in a bowl. Using an electric mixer on medium-high speed, cream the butter and sugar together until light and fluffy. Beat in the poppy seeds and lemon zest and continue to beat until thoroughly combined.

# Any-Berry Butter

### Serves 4 to 6

*1 cup unsalted butter, at room temperature*
*2 tablespoons confectioners' sugar, plus more as needed*
*1/2 cup fresh or thawed frozen raspberries, strawberries, or blueberries*

Place the butter and sugar in a bowl. Using an electric mixer on medium-high speed, cream the butter and sugar together until light and fluffy. On low speed, blend in the berries until just combined into the mixture. Stir in additional sugar if the berries are too tart.

# Almond Butter

_Serves 4 to 6_

*1 cup unsalted butter, at room temperature*
*3 tablespoons confectioners' sugar*
*³/4 cup toasted, slivered almonds, pulverized in a food
    processor or blender*
*¹/8 teaspoon pure almond extract*

Place the butter and sugar in a bowl. Using an electric mixer
on medium-high speed, cream the butter and sugar together
until light and fluffy. On low speed, blend in the almonds and
almond extract until just combined into the mixture.

# About the Authors

STEVE SIEGELMAN was one of the original cooks at Bette's Diner and is now a Berkeley-based writer. He has written or contributed to ten cookbooks, including *Firehouse Food: Cooking with San Francisco's Firefighters.* His television writing credits include "Mexico One Plate at a Time" with Rick Bayless, and "Mario Eats Italy" with Mario Batali. Steve once heated the last tortilla in the house for James Beard and was so nervous, he burned it. Fortunately, Mr. Beard was distracted by admirers and forgot that he had ever ordered it.

BETTE KROENING is one of the founders of the Diner and the namesake of the place. These days, she spends most of her time managing the business, but her roots are in cooking. Bette once served potato pancakes to Senator Jacob Javits, whose daughter, Carla, worked at the Diner. Five years later, Bette almost burned down the Jacob Javits Center in New York City when she sparked an electrical fire after plugging in too many pancake griddles in her booth at the Fancy Food Show.

Eleven years after cofounding the Diner, SUE CONLEY went on to a new life as a West Marin cowgirl and pioneer in the artisan cheese movement through her companies, Cowgirl Creamery, Tomales Bay Foods, and Artisan Cheese. Sue once found herself seated in a white stretch limo across from Tammy Wynette, who was carefully applying pancake makeup in preparation for an appearance on "The Dolly Parton Show."

# Bette's Diner Products

All of our pancake and scone mixes are made with all-natural, freshly milled flours. They are available in specialty food stores across the country or by mail order direct from our warehouse. A 16-ounce bag makes 25 to 30 (4-inch) pancakes or 9 to 12 (8-inch) waffles.

- Classic Buttermilk Pancake and Waffle Mix: A proven hit at the Diner. (16 ounces)

- Oatmeal Pancake and Waffle Mix: Whole oats give these pancakes a nutty, sweet flavor. (16 ounces)

- Buckwheat Pancake and Waffle Mix: A longstanding health food, buckwheat flour gives these pancakes a distinctive, tangy flavor. (16 ounces)

- Raisin Scone Mix: Our original, award-winning scone mix. This mix makes moist, creamy scones every time. (16 ounces)

- Lemon Currant Scone Mix: The perfect scone with morning coffee, afternoon tea, or as a biscuit with dinner. Our most versatile flavor. (16 ounces)

- Orange Cranberry Scone Mix: Produces a sweet, wholesome scone. Dried cranberries add sparkle to this Diner favorite. (16 ounces)

For more information call (510) 644-3932.
To order by mail or online: Bette's Oceanview Diner,
1807 Fourth Street,
Berkeley, California 94710
www.bettesdiner.com

# Index